Enjoy the walks, and may the sun shine all day, your boots feel comfortable on your feet and your pack feels as light as a feather! Happy walking!
John N. Merrill

Something to ponder.

As we walk around this amazing world, we take for granted the stunning diversity of life and nature. We pass the slopes of mountains and the river valleys. We see birds, insects, animals and all the kaleidoscope of flowers and trees. But let's stop for a moment and just stand in awe of this plethora of sights. However hard we as humans try, we cannot match the magnificence that our eyes see. Whether you are spiritual or not, you cannot ignore or be moved to wonder at the incredible work of a higher dimension - the divine.

While many would say this is evolution, there still has be "someone", who first thought up the flower, tree, bird, animal, and landscape. You only have to gaze at a small mountain flower and see the delicate stems and petals made to perfection. Whilst the earth's movement have created our landscape, the forces of the divine have been at work to help create that breathtaking view. We on the other-hand have been given eyes and feelings, so that we can appreciate and stand in awe at the sight before us.

So as we wander down a path in woodland or high mountains, where the whole spectrum of life is laid out for us to see. Lets give eternal thanks for being able to walk and see these things first hand. To be able to touch, feel and appreciate the work of the divine, makes the effort more than worthwhile. So, as you walk, stop and ponder at the never ending variety of sights and smells that confront us on each stride we take.

John N. Merrill 2014

WALKING THE PURE WAY

I believe a walk, whatever the distance, should be done on two feet, with basics of life on your back and map/gps in your hand. When I first started the thought of missing a section and using transport was the death knoll to the walk. I could not live with myself if I had missed a section.

Today when I walk to Santiago de Compestella on a 1,000 mile route, I am saddened that many walkers take a bus here and there, missing out a section that was "boring". I could never understand, at first, having overtook a walker, a few days later they were ahead of me. They had certainly not passed me. When I walked the Pacific Crest Trail in America. I walked it all despite deep snow in the Sierra's. Many who get there because of snow and closed trails, bus round, missing 300 miles or more of trail. I had snow and had to walk beneath the mountains for four days before finding a way in. It still meant that I had full-filled my plan and walked from Mexico to Canada un-aided. And having reached Canada flew back to the High Sierra's and climbed them all. Then I went home feeling complete.'

Similarly on the Appalachian Trail, on reaching a Post Office where my food parcel was, I loaded my pack with 14 days of food and basics and headed back into the wilderness and emerged 14 days later at another Post Office and parcel. Today, few do it traditionally, opting to carry 3 days of food and hike & hitch-hike out to a food store. Makes no sense physically and mentally, and makes the walk twice as long.

Sadly today sport is tainted with performance enhancing drugs. I have never taken any drug, only half a dozen aspirins over the years, and never seen a doctor. To excel there is one simple method. Be totally devoted and singleminded at your sport and whilst getting to peak performance realise that it is not just physical but having the correct mindset to do it.

I walk for it is the most natural and life enhancing activity you can do. Plus there is never any age limit; you can still walk when you are a hundred. So walk naturally one foot in front of the other and enjoy the landscape and before you know it you are at your destination, regardless of the mileage and mountains on the way. Glow with pride at making it on your own feet all the way and in an untainted way.

Revd. John N. Merrill - May 2017.

The John Merrill Foundation

Short Circular walks in the Epping Forest District

By Revd. John N. Merrill

"Hiking the sacred paths & trails of the world for others to follow."

THE JOHN MERRILL FOUNDATION

THE JOHN MERRILL FOUNDATION
32, Holmesdale, Waltham Cross,
Hertfordshire, England. EN8 8QY

Tel/Fax - 01992-762776

E-mail - john@johnmerrillwalkguides.co.uk

www.johnmerrillwalkguides.co.uk

www.thejohnmerrillministry.co.uk

www.londoninterfaithchurch.co.uk

A catalogue record for this book is available from the British Library.

Conceived, edited, typset and designed by *The John Merrill Foundation*
Printed and handmade by *John N. Merrill.*
Book layout and cover design by *John N. Merrill*

© Text and photographs - by Revd. John N. Merrill 2013
© Maps by Revd. John N. Merrill, HonMUniv, R.I.M.A. 2013
© Additional material - Revd. John N. Merrill, HonMUniv, 2013.

ISBN 978 - 0-9564644-4-6
First Published - April 2010. Reprinted and revised - April 2013.
Special limited edition.

Typeset in Humanst521 - bold, italic, and plain 11pt, 14pt and 18pt
Main titles in 18pt .**Humanst521 Bd BT** by John Merrill in Adobe Pagemaker on a iMac.

Please note - *The maps in this guide are purely illustrative. You are encouraged to use the appropriate 1:25,000 O.S. Explorer map as detailed on each walk.*

John Merrill confirms he has walked all the routes in this book and detailed what he found. Meticulous research has been undertaken to ensure that this publication is highly accurate at the time of going to press. The publishers, however, cannot be held responsible for alterations, errors, omissions, or for changes in details given. They would welcome information to help keep the book up to date.

The John Merrill Foundation maintains the John Merrill Library and archives and administers the worldwide pubishing rights of John Merrill's works in all media formats.

Printed on paper from a 100% sustainable forest.
The John Merrill Foundation plants sufficient trees through the
Woodland Trust to replenish the trees used in its publications.

A little about Revd. John N. Merrill

John is unique, possessing the skills of a marathon runner, mountain climber and athlete. Since his first 1,000 mile walk through the islands of the Inner and Outger Hebrides in 1970, he has since walked over 218,000 miles and worn out 132 paits of boots, 49 rucksacks and more than 1,600 pairs of socks. He has brought marathon walking to Olympic standard. In 1978 he became the first person to walk around the entire coastline of Britain - 7,000 miles. He has walked across Europe, the Alps and Pyrenees - 3,000 miles with 600,000 feet of ascent and descent. In America he has walked the 2,500 mile Appalachian Trail; the Pacific Crest Trail - 2,500 miles in record time; the Continental Divide Trail; became the first person to thru-hike the Buckeye Trail - 1,350 miles in Ohio and completed a unique 4,260 mile walk in 178 days coast to coast across America. He has climbed all the mountains in New Mexico and walked all the trails.

In Britain he has walked all the National Trails many times; linked all the National Parks and trails in a 2,060 mile walk; completed a 1,608 mile Land's End to John o' Groats walk and countless other unique walks. He has walked three times to Santiago de Compostella via different routes; to St. Olav's Shrine in Norway - 420 miles; walked to Assisi, St. Gilles du Gard, the Cathar Ways and to Mont St. Michel. He has walked every long distance path in France and Germany, and walked to every pilgrimage destination in England and France, and extensively walked in every country in Europe.

He has walked in Africa; all the trails in the Hong Kong Islands; and completed five trekking expeditions to the Himalyas and India. Not only is he the world's leading marathon walker he is Britain's most experienced walker. John is author of more than 440 walk guides which have sold more than 4 million copies with more than 1 million sold on the Peak District. He has created more than 80 challenge walks which have been used to raise, so far, more than a £1 million for different charities.

John has never broken a bone or been lost and never had any trouble anywhere. He still walks in the same body he was born with, has had no replacements and does not use poles. This he puts down to his deep spiritual nature and in 2010 he was ordained as a multi-faith Minister - a universal monk, *"honouring and embracing all faiths and none"*. He conducts weddings and funerals, teaches Qigong and is a Reiki practioner. He gives talks all over the UK.

Loughton Camp in Epping Forest.

CONTENTS

Greensted Log Church.

INTRODUCTION

It all began with a log church and a new friend who told me she came from Chipping Ongar. *"Where's that"*, I asked. *"Near Epping"*, she replied. Later that day I looked at the Ordnance Survey map and located both places. I set off the next week and walked to the oldest log church church in the world at Greensted and passed through Chipping Ongar on my circuit. I was hooked and wondered why I had missed this part of Essex so close to my home.

Over the next two months I began exploring the area within the boundaries of Epping Forest District Council. I knew Epping Forest well, but much the area was all new territory to me. And what a delight it has been to discover such fine quiet walking, full of history so close to London. I kept away from paths I knew - see my book on *"Short Circular walks in Epping Forest"* - and first began to explore Chipping Ongar and the villages of Fyfield and Moreton. I noticed the ruins of Latton Priory on the map and did a walk from Epping Green to it. Further north was Matching, and I spent an amazing day exploring the surrounding villages, full of unique history and surrounded by quiet "High Country", where sheep roam. I returned later, to find the former Matching Airfield.

Continuing my wartime explorations I walked around North Weald and found many fascinating features. Another walk took me to Ongar Park and more remains of the defence of North Weald airfield. I had done a previous walk from Abridge and using new paths followed a Roman Road and passed Hill House, a secluded gem. To the south I complete a walk from Waltham Abbey to Warlies Park; another gem and whose house is a stunning piece of architecture.

My final walk was around Loughton, using Epping Forest and Theydon Bois. Although the longest in the book at 12 miles, it is a delight and follows the River Roding for awhile. So, here are twelve walks of various lengths that fully explore the area and bring you you to an incredible diverse array of rural walking and amazing buildings, churches and history. Set off for yourself and explore this area of Essex, for it has much to offer the walker.

Happy walking

Alan W Merual

ABOUT THE WALKS

Whilst every care is taken detailing and describing the walks ikn this book, it should be borne in mind that the countryside changes witgh the seasons and the work of man. I have described the walks to the best of my ability, detailing what I have found actually on the walk in the way of stiles, kissing gates and signs. You should always walk with the appropriate O.S. map as detailed for each walk; open on the walk area for constant reference, or downladed onto your mobile phone. Obviously with the passage of time stiles become broken or replaced by kissing gates; inns change their name or have close down. Signs have a habit of being broken or pushed over and often they are pointing in the wrong direction! All the routes follow public rights of way and only rarely will you find a tree blown down across the path or an electric fence, requiring a small detour. Some rights of way are rerouted such as around a farm but they are generally well signed.

All rights of way have colour coded arrows on marker posts, stiles, gates, path posts, trees and these help you showing the direction of travel.

YELLOW - Public footpath.
BLUE - Public bridleway.
RED - Byway open to all traffic (BOAT).
BLACK - Road used as a public path (RUPP).
WHITE - Concessionary and Permissive path.

The seasons bring occasional problems whilst out walking which should also be borne in mind. In the height of summer the paths become overgrown and you may have to fight your way through in a few places. In low lying areas the fields are full of crops. Usually a defined path leads through. In summer the ground is usually dry but in autumn and winter can be wet and slippery.

The mileage for each walk is based on several calculations -
1. My pedometer reading and steps taken - usually 2,000 to a mile.
2. The route on the map measured.
3. The time I took for the walk - the average person walks at 3mph - 2.5mph uphill.

Allow 20 mins for a mile; 10 mins for 1/2 mile and 5 mins for 1/4 mile.

"For every mile that you walk you extend your life by 21 mins."

HOW TO DO A WALK

The walk in this book follows a public right of way, be it a footpath, bridleway, Boat or RUPP, which are marked in green lines on the Ordnance Survey 1:25,000 Explorer maps.

On each section I have detailed which map is needed and I would urge you to carry and use the map. As I walk I always have the map out on the section I am walking, constantly checking that I am walking the right way. Also when coming to any road or path junction, I can check on the map to ensure I take the right route.

Most the paths are signed and waymarked with coloured arrows but I would at best describe them as intermittent. They act as confirmation of the right of way you are walking and the arrow points in the direction of travel.

The countryside has the added problem of vandalism and you will find path logo's and Information Boards spray painted over and path signs pointing the wrong way! That is why I always advise carrying the map open on the area you are walking to check you are walking the right way. In my walking instructions I have given the name of each main and minor road, canal lock, and bridge, together with the house numbers where you turn and the name of inns passed. All to help you have a smooth and trouble free walk.

I confirm I have walked every route and written what I found at the time of walking.

These comments are not meant to put you off but to make you aware of some of the problems of walking in the countryside.

The Art of walking the John Merrill Way.

1. Always set off in the clothes you plan to wear all day, given the weather conditions. Only on sudden changes in the weather will I stop and put on a waterproof or warmer clothing.

2. Set off at a steady comfortable pace, which you can maintain all day. You should end the walk as fresh as when you started.

3. Maintain your pace and don't stop. Stopping for any period of time disrupts your rythmn and takes upwards of a mile (20 mins) to settle back down into the flow/ease of movement.

4. Switch your phone off. Listen and enjoy the countryside - the smell of the flowers, bird song, the rustle of leaves and the tinkling stream, and observe the wildlife.

5. Ignore the mileage and ascents - don't tick the miles or hills, just concentrate on what the walk's goal is. To think otherwise slows you down and makes the walk a struggle rather than a joy. In a similar vein, when ascending just keep a steady pace and keep going. To stop is to disrupt the flow and make the ascent interminable.

6. Whist a walk is a challenge to complete, it is not just exercise. You should enjoy the world around you, the flowers, birds, wildlife and nature and look at and explore the historical buildings and churches that you pass. Industrial complex's have their own beauty. All are part of life's rich tapestry.

7. Remember that for every mile you walk, you extend your life by 21 minutes.

8. A journey of a 1,000 miles begins with a single step and a mile requires 2,000 strides.

"The expert traveller leaves no footprints" Lao Tzu.

EQUIPMENT NOTES

Today there is a bewildering variety of walking gear, much is superfluous to general walking in Britain. As a basic observation, people over dress for the outdoors. Basically equipment should be serviceable and do the task. I don't use walking poles; humans were built to walk with two legs! The following are some of my thoughts gathered from my walking experiences.

BOOTS - For summer use and day walking I wear lightweight boots. For high mountains and longer trips I prefer a good quality boot with a full leather upper, of medium weight, traditional style ,with a vibram sole. I always add a foam cushioned insole to help cushion the base of my feet.

SOCKS - I generally wear two thick pairs as this helps minimise blisters. The inner pair are of loop stitch variety and approximately 80% wool. The outer are also a thick pair of approximately 80% wool. I often wear double inner socks, which minimise blisters.

CLOTHES & WATERPROOFS - for general walking I wear a T shirt or cotton shirt with a cotton wind jacket on top, and shorts - even in snow! You generate heat as you walk and I prefer to layer my clothes to avoid getting too hot. Depending on the season will dictate how many layers you wear. In soft rain I just use my wind jacket for I know it quickly dries out. In heavy or consistent rain I slip on a poncho, which covers me and my pack and allows air to circulate, while keeping me dry. Only in extreme conditions will I don over-trousers, much preferring to get wet and feel comfortable. I never wear gaiters, except when cross country skiing, or in snow and glacier crossings. I find running shorts and sleeveless T shirts ideal for summer.

FOOD - as I walk I carry bars of chocolate, for they provide instant energy and are light to carry. In winter a flask of hot coffee is welcome. I never carry water and find no hardship from not doing so, but this is a personal matter! From experience I find the more I drink the more I want and sweat. You should always carry some extra food such as trail mix & candy bars etc., for emergencies. Full milk is a very underestimated source of food and liquid.

RUCKSACKS - for day walking I use a rucksack of about 30/40 litre capacity and although it leaves excess space it does mean that the sac is well padded, with an internal frame and padded shoulder straps, chest strap and waist strap. Inside apart from the basics for one day, in winter I carry gloves, wear a hat/cap and carry a spare pullover and a pair of socks.

MAP & COMPASS - when I am walking I always have the relevant map - preferably 1:25,000 scale - open in my hand. This enables me to constantly check that I am walking the right way. In case of bad weather I carry a compass, which once mastered gives you complete confidence in thick cloud or mist - you should always know where you are; I have a built in direction finder! Map reading and compass work is a skill and should be learnt. With modern technology you can now downloaded OS maps to your phone, record your walk, mileage, calories, steps taken, walking speed and time taken.

FOLLOW THE COUNTRY CODE

* Be safe - plan ahead and follow any signs.

* Leave gates and property
as you find them.

* Protect plants and animals, and take
your litter home.

* Keep dogs
under close control.

* Consider
other people.

* Take only photographs,
leave only footprints.

A pause for thought.....

The Ten Indian Commandments -

Treat the earth and all that dwell thereon with respect.

Remain close to the Great Spirit.

Show great respect for your fellow beings.

Work together for the benefit of all mankind.

Give assistance and kindness wherever needed.

Do what you know to be right.

Look after the well-being of mind and body.

Dedicate a share of your efforts to the greater good.

Be truthful and honest at all times.

Take full responsibility for your actions.

MATCHING GREEN & HIGH LAVER - 9 1/2 MILES

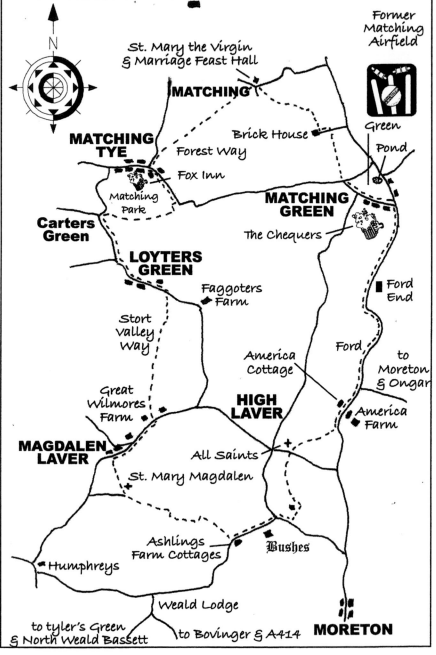

Former Matching Airfield

St. Mary the Virgin & Marriage Feast Hall

MATCHING

Brick House

Green

Pond

MATCHING TYE

Forest Way

Fox Inn

Matching Park

MATCHING GREEN

Carters Green

The Chequers

LOYTERS GREEN

Faggoters Farm

Ford End

Stort Valley Way

America Cottage

Ford

to Moreton & Ongar

Great Wilmores Farm

HIGH LAVER

America Farm

MAGDALEN LAVER

All Saints

St. Mary Magdalen

Ashlings Farm Cottages

Bushes

Humphreys

Weald Lodge

to Tyler's Green & North Weald Bassett

to Bovinger & A414

MORETON

MATCHING GREEN
& HIGH LAVER
- 9 1/2 MILES
- allow 4 hours

Basic route - Matching Green - Ford End - Ford - America Cottage & Farm House - All Saints, High Laver - Bushes - Ashlings Farm Cottages - St, Mary Magdalen - Magdalen Laver - Great Wilmores Farm - Stort Valley Way - Loyters Green - Carters Green - Matching Park - Matching Tye - Matching - Brick House - Matching Green.

Map - O.S. 1:25,000 Explorer Series No. - 183 - Chelmsford & The Rodings.

Car Park & Start - Beside the Green in Matching Green. Alternative starts from small parking areas at All Saints, High Laver and St. Mary Magdalen, Magdalen Laver.

Inns - The Fox Inn, Matching Tye. The Chequers, Matching Green.

ABOUT THE WALK - A walk full of diverse interest with a surprise every mile! This is the "High Country" of the area where sheep roam. Leaving Matching Green you follow a single tracked lane to a ford and past America Cottage, whose country name will become evident at All Saints church, High Laver. Soon after you pass the superlative example of Tudor work at Bushes. Quiet paths lead across the fields to St. Mary Magdalen, where you join a section of the Stort Valley Way. Now heading north to Matching Tye and then eastwards to Matching and your first inn. The church here has a memorial plaque to the American bomber squadron that was based near Matching Green in World War 2. Beside the church is a unique Tudor building, built in c1480, as a wedding feast hall. One mile later you are back in Matching Green with a cricket green and an inn.

WALKING INSTRUCTIONS - Starting from The Chequers Inn in Matching Green, walk along the road, eastwards to the road junction opposite Albion

House. Turn right along the road, signed Matching School, and keep right. Pass houses and the school and the road now becomes a single tracked lane. In 1/2 mile pass Ford End on the left. Continue ahead as the road loops round to the ford - no footbridge, but wadeable. Follow the road to the junction with the turning for Little Laver, Moreton & Ongar. Keep straight ahead and pass America Cottage on the right and America Farmhouse on the left; the American name will be understood at High Laver. Just after America Farmhouse the road curves left, here on the right is a footpath sign. Turn right onto it and keep the hedge on your right to a footbridge and stile. Here turn half right and keep a stream on your left to a stile. Cross the next field, diagonally left, well to the left of All Saints church, High Laver, to a footpath sign, stile and road. You route is directly opposite - footpath sign and stile. But first turn right to visit All Saints church. On the right of the porch is a tomb and monument to John Locke, whose philosophy led to the founding of the United States of America.

Bushes, an exceptionally fine wooden building.

Cross the road to the stile and footpath sign. First, keep a hedge on your left as you walk in sheep country. Next is an open field and descend, aiming for the far lefthand corner with a path post. You are aiming for the lefthand side of a building with tall chimneys - High Laver House. At the field edge turn left and then right over a stile. Keep to the righthand path to a large gate and stile, by a footpath post and reach a road. Turn right and pass the entrance to High Laver House. Moments later turn left along the road signed - North Weald and Epping. In a short distance pass the Tudor house, Bushes, on the left. Continue along the road to Ashlings Farm Cottages, where the road turn left. Keep right as footpath signed, along the path beside the field edge and ditch on the left. Reaching a line of trees, turn left and 100 metres later, right and cross an open field to a hedge end. Turn right and soon left to cross another open field, aiming for the prominent tower of St. Mary Magdalen church. At the other side of the reach a path post and footbridge. Cross and continue to the church.

Walk through the lefthand side of the churchyard to a kissing gate. Continue across the field on a defined path to the road at Magdalen Laver/ Tilegate Green. Turn right and keep right past Tilegate; you are now following the Stort Valley Way. Soon after and before Great Wilmores Farm, turn left as path signed. The path is well signed and soon bear right and a green path with a hedge on the left. 1/2 mile later cross footbridges to an open field. As arrowed go straight across to a footbridge and path sign; basically aiming to the right of a yellow cream painted house, and gain Faggotters Lane - a single track lane.

Turn left and pass Little Faggotters on the left. Soon after Laughing Barn. Follow the lane right and soon after keep ahead with New Way Lane on the left. Follow the road sign - To Carters Green and Matching Tye. Pass White Cottage on the right. At the next junction turn right - signed Matching Tye. The road then turns left at Hoggs Farm, immediately after turn right onto a track which doubles back on itself to pass a granary on the left. Bear right, as signed, and walk along the edge of woodland - Matching Park - walking along a grass path. At its eastern end turn left then right along the field edge to gain a footbridge and road. Turn left and pass The Manse, Mathew Chapel (Built by Joseph Mathew in 1875 and now a private house), to reach Matching Tye and the Fox Inn. On the right is Gainsborough Cottage (1692).

Turn right along the road to Hillcrest on the left. Turn right, as footpath signed both the Stort Valley Way and Forest Way. The path is basically dead straight by the hedge and ditch on the right, along the field edge. In little over 1/2 mile reach the road in Matching. Turn right to reach the Wedding Feast Hall and St. Mary the Virgin church., on the left; opposite is Matching Hall. Walk past the church porch to the road. Cross to another path sign; here you leave the Stort Valley Way and Forest Way. The path keeps to the edge of the field on the right to a stile. Continue a little left and then turn left and later right as you aim for the lefthand side of Brick House. Keep left and reach the farm drive. Turn left and in a few metres, right, to follow the path along the edge of the field and past the football field to the road beside Wingates. Turn left and then right along the road for Moreton and Ongar and reach the green of Matching Green. Keep left along the edge of the green to reach The Chequers Inn where you began.

MATCHING GREEN - Near the Chequers Inn a house has a blue plaque to Augusta Edwin John 1878 - Painter who lived here. His best known paintings are *"Going down to the sea"* and *"The Orange Jacket"*. The site of Matching Airfield is 2 miles away and is signed - see separate section..

HIGH LAVER - On the right of the porch of All Saints church can be seen the tomb and plaque of John Locke, English philosopher 1632 - 1704. Among his written works are, Essay of Human Understandings; Letters of Toleration and Notes upon St. Paul's Epistles to the Galatians, Corinthians, Romans and Ephesians.

MAGDALEN LAVER - St. Mary Magdalen Church dates back to the 12th. century. The wooden tower is mostly 16th. century, with some of the wood dated a century earlier. Beside the porch is an unusually fine tomb to William Cole, Sheriff of Essex, who died in 1730. Inside the timber roof with two Queen Posts.

STORT VALLEY WAY - 28 mile (45 km) walk around harlow, via the River Stort Navigation, Sawbridgeworth, Sheering, Matching, Magdalen Laver and Epping Green. The walk logo is a dragonfly. Starts and ends at Roydon GR. TL406105.

Gainsborough Cottage (1692), Matching Tye.

MATCHING TYE - The word Tye means a settlement around a common or green. The central part of the village is a conservation area, with Gainsborough Cottage a fine building.

THE FOREST WAY - A signed path linking Epping Forest with Hadfield Forest. 25 miles (40 km). Starts from Loughton Station, Essex GR. TQ423956. Ends Hatfield Forest Country Park GR. TL534213. Signed with Tree and name on a green background.

MATCHING - The Marriage Feast Room was built in c1480 by William Chimney. *"Built for the entertainment of poor people on their wedding day"* It is still in use today. The upper floor is one large room with a crown post roof. For awhile the lower part was used as an almshouse and school. Today there is a very active Friends of the Feast House, preserving a unique feature of village life. Matching Hall is mostly 17th. century.

St. Mary the Virgin church; the parish church of Matching Green, originates from Norman times. The nave is 13th. century but much of the church was restored in 1875. The tower is 15th. century, as is the font.

MATCHING AIRFIELD

In preparation for D Day an airfield was made close to Matching Green. Work began in 1942 and continued for 15 months, clearing the area, levelling and using rubble from bombed houses in East London as hardcore; the base was operational in 1944. The 391st Bomb Group of the U. S. Airforce from Tampa, Florida were based here flying Marauders. They provided tactical support before and after the D Day landings. Bombing airfields, bridges, railways and roads. They flew 6,000 sorties and 197 American airmen were either killed, wounded and missing during this time. By late 1944 the airmen were based in France and the RAF used the base for training and as part of the final push in 1945. After the war the base was returned to arable land and only a control tower, hangers and memorial plaque remain today. A monument can be seen in Matching church - see below.

Photo © www.military-aircraft.org.uk

Martin B-26 Marauder - A high speed long range twin engined bomber which could carry a load of 2,000 pounds. The first plane was built in November 1940 and some 5,000 were eventually built. The plane was 58 feet 3 inches long, with a wingspan of 71 feet. Operated by a crew of seven. Overall the bombers were involved in 129,943 missions, dropping 169,382 tons of bombs.

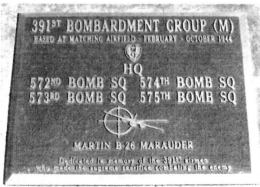

23

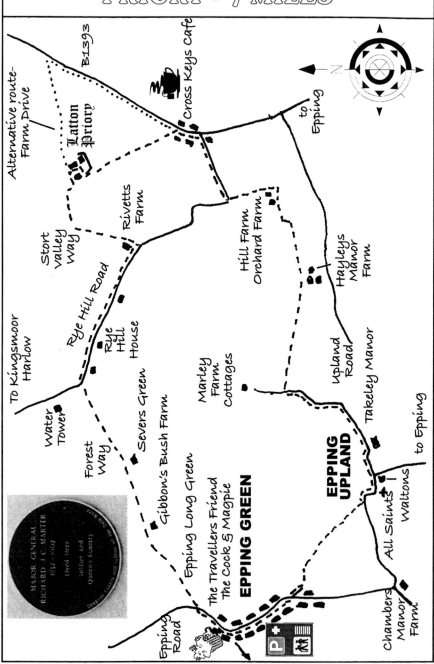

EPPING GREEN
& LATTON PRIORY
- 7 MILES
- allow 3 hours

Basic route - Epping Green - Epping Long Green - Forest Way - Severs Green - Rye Hill Road - Rivetts farm - Latton Priory - Thornwood Common - Orchard Farm - Marles Farm Drive - Epping Upland - Epping Green.

Map - O.S. 1:25,000 Explorer Series No. - 174 - Epping Forest & Lee Valley.

Car Park & Start - Limited roadside parking in Epping Green.

Inns - The Travellers Friend and The Cock & Magpie; Epping Green.

Cafe - Cross Keys Cafe, beside the B1393.

ABOUT THE WALK - The principal aim of this walk is to see the remains of Latton Priory - a former Augustinian priory and one of the few monastic sites in this area. First you follow the Epping Long Green (Corporation of London property, as is Epping Forest). This grassy path is also part of the Stort Valley Way and Forest Way. A road walk at Rye Hill brings you to the path to the priory. The remains of the church, with high arches can be seen, together with a moat. The path from here to the B1393, Epping Road, is not waymarked, but is straight forward. There is an alternative road walk here, as detailed. From the B1393 you pick up good paths from Orchard Farm to Epping Upland. Here is the former Epping parish church - All Saints, and the former home of a Queen Victoria Equerry - Major General Richard J. C. Marter (1832-1902). The final path leads across the fields to Epping Green with two inns. A pleasant walk around the quiet high ground - some of the highest parts of Essex - between Epping and Harlow.

There is limited roadside parking in Epping Green. Possible parking area at the start of the Epping Long Green.

WALKING INSTRUCTIONS - Starting from Epping Green walk beside the Epping Road, northwards, and pass the Cock & Magpie Inn and Travellers Friend on the left. Follow the road right, passing a pond and the Epping Green Chapel on the right. Soon after the road curves left, here on the right is a bar gate. Turn right past this and onto another and drive to Summers Farm. Cross to the footpath sign - Epping Long Green (Part of Epping Forest; Corporation of London). For little over a mile you follow this grassy swathe path, mostly with a hedge on your left. In 1/4 mile pass the solitary house on the right - Gibbons Bush Farm. Less than a 1/4 mile later is Severs Green on the right. Continue ahead and in a 1/3 mile reach the Rye Hill Road, to your left is a tall prominent water Tower. Turn right along the usually quite road for 3/4 mile.

First past Wayside and then Rye Hill House and then Whipps Cottage before reaching Rivetts Farm on the left. Immediately past it, turn left, as path signed and still on the Stort Valley way. Follow the hedged path for 1/4 mile to its end and turn right on a track; ahead can be seen the prominent "church" of Latton Priory. The track curves right towards the buildings; here the Stort Valley Way turns left. Continue to the buildings, and turn left then right through the farm towards the house. On the left is the former church, with tall arches, and now used a tall square barn.

Note - *The path from here to the B1393 Epping Road, is little used, but you simply keep straight ahead. If you want a longer easier route, follow the farm drive; right of way, to the B1393 road and turn right, along the pavement for more than 1/2 mile to the Cross Keys Cafe and houses and road junction of the Rye Hill Road. Both routes meet near here.*

Infront of the farm house turn right and then left to a gate. Keep the water filled moat on your left, then fence. The path line is now dead straight. At the end of the fence, where it turns left, keep straight ahead across the open field to a woodland strip. Keep straight through and cross the next field on the same trajectory to gate and footpath sign beside the B1393 road. Turn right and immediately pass the Cross Keys Cafe and reach houses and the road on the right, signed - Rye Hill 1 mile.

Turn right along Rye Hill Road; you walked along upper part of the road earlier. In 1/4 mile the road turns sharp right; here turn left, as footpath signed and walk beside the hedge on the right. On the other side is the farm drive to

Orchard Farm. Follow the hedge as it loops around the farm to a footbridge on the right. Turn right across it and on past Hill Farm to a stile. Continue ahead to a path post and turn left and a few metres later right at the next post. Cross the open field and descend gently to pass an industrial farm complex to your left (Hayes Manor Farm). The path now becomes better defined as you continue to a stile and along a grassy swathe in woodland to another stile. Continue to a footbridge and keep straight ahead on a path along the edge of the field with a stream/ditch on your left. Continue to a path sign and the farm drive to Marles Farm and Cottages. Turn left and ascend gently along the drive which swings right and left. Follow it right as it now becomes a road - Upland Road - and pass Takeley Manor on the left as you enter Epping Upland.

At the road junction with the Epping Road, keep ahead and pass Waltons house on the left, then All Saints church. The road - Greenwood Road - turns sharp right and left. Here on the lefthand corner leave the road, as path signed. Follow the path across the field to a post (many people walk around the field edge on this path). Keep ahead and descend slightly to a footbridge. Ascend to the field edge and path post. Turn left and soon right into Pump Lane. Keep right along it to the main road, passing the water pump on the left at the junction. Turn right and follow the road back into Epping Green past the shops on the right to the Cock & Magpie Inn.

THE FOREST WAY - 25 miles (40 km) - Links Epping Forest and Hatfield Forest together.

STORT VALLEY WAY - 28 miles (45 km) - Starts and ends at Roydon, Essex. All within Essex, as it includes Sheering, the River Stort, Matching, Magdalen Laver and Epping Green.

LATTON PRIORY, listed building - Mentioned in the Domesday Book - "lattuna". Founded in the 12th. century for Augustinian Canons. At the end of the 13th. century there was a Prior and two canons. Closed in 1534 with just a prior. The Priory church was rebuilt in the 14th. century and includes Roman brick and Reigate stone. Today only the four crossing arches remain, with parts of the south and north transept still visible. The chancel site is now occupied by a barn. Part of the farm building - south wall - is believed to the wall of the frater. The moat, which is visible is partly filled in. Within its area is a fish pond. The whole site was used between 1066 to 1539 AD.

Latton Priory.

MAJOR GENERAL
RICHARD J. C. MARTER
1832 – 1902

Lived Here

Soldier and
Queen's Equerry

Dragoon Guards and soldier of the Zulu Wars

Waltons ,
Epping Upland -
Plaque to Major General
Marter.

ALL SAINTS CHURCH, EPPING UPLAND - The original parish church of Epping - *"The people on the upland."* Medieval with a 13th. century nave and tower. Its origins go back to Norman times and was extensively restored in 1878. The present parish church in Epping, is dedicated to St. John.

EPPING GREEN - The Cock & Magpie inn dates from the 18th. century, but was not an inn until Victorian times. The village pond was originally the blacksmiths cooling pond. The Epping Long Green Lane is a former cattle drover road.

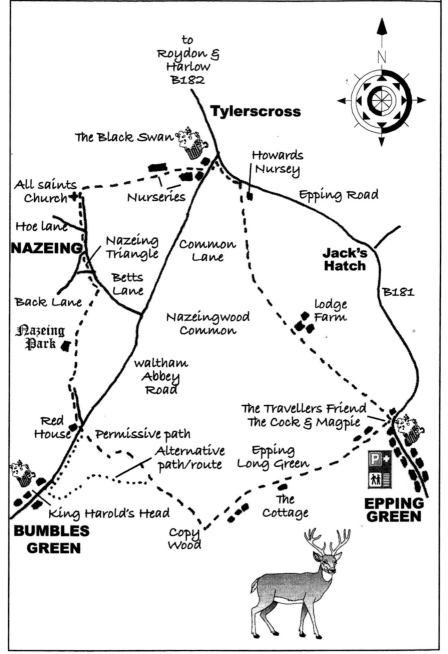

EPPING GREEN & NAZEING - 5 1/2 MILES

N

to Roydon & Harlow B182

Tylerscross

The Black Swan

Howards Nursey

All saints Church

Nurseries

Epping Road

Hoe lane

NAZEING

Nazeing Triangle

Common Lane

Jack's Hatch

Betts Lane

B181

Back Lane

Nazeingwood Common

lodge Farm

Nazeing Park

waltham Abbey Road

The Travellers Friend
The Cock & Magpie

Red House

Permissive path

Alternative path/route

Epping Long Green

EPPING GREEN

King Harold's Head

The Cottage

BUMBLES GREEN

Copy Wood

EPPING GREEN AND NAZEING
- 5 1/2 MILES
- allow 2 1/2 hours

Basic route - Epping Green - Lodge Farm - Tylerscross - Nazeing Church (All saints) - Nazeing - Nazeing Park - Bumbles Green - Copy Wood - Epping Long Green - Epping Green.

Map - O.S. 1:25,000 Explorer Series No. - 174 - Epping Forest & Lee Valley.

Car Park & Start - Limited parking between the Cock & Magpie Inn and the Travellers Friend, beside the B181 on the northern side of Epping Green; at the end of the Epping Long Green. Alternative parking at Nazeing church; approximately halfway.

Inns - The Travellers Friend and The Cock & Magpie, Epping Green. The Black Swan, Tylerscross. King Harold's Head, Bumbles Green.

ABOUT THE WALK - A surprisingly hilly walk! First you descend to Lodge Farm and onto Tylerscross. Then you pass nurseries and keep to high ground, with views, to reach Nazeing church. Soon you are descending again through Nazeing Park to the road near Bumbles Green. Soon after, you are ascending once again, to Copy Wood, and gain the level Epping Long Green, back to Epping Green. A short walk full of surprises and extensive views. As I began the ascent to Copy Wood I watched the largest herd - thirty - fallow deer that I have ever seen in this area; you never know what lies around the corner; that is the joy of walking. You walk sections of the Three Forest Way and Stort Valley Way and pass several well spaced out inns!

The walk can be added to Latton Priory Walk, making a 13 mile long figure of eight walk. You follow a permissive path after Nazeing Park and this can be avoided by walking along the road to Bumbles Green - wide verge - and then

31

following a right of way which joins the permissive path. This adds 1/2 mile to the walk. At the time of writing, the path was well signed but the gate was padlocked and had to be climbed over.

WALKING INSTRUCTIONS - Starting from the Travellers Friend, immediately after it where the road turns right, on the left is a path sign - Lodge Farm 0.8 km. Follow this fence and hedged path and keep straight ahead, soon you begin to descend with a hedge on your left. As you do so you have extensive views northwards; you are also following a section of the Three Forests Way. In 1/2 mile reach Lodge Farm and keep to the lefthand side of it to the farm drive. Immediately after bear slightly right, as footpath signed and follow a track which soon swings left and right. Continue ahead and cross three small footbridges. Cross another path and as footpath post indicated continue ahead and reach Epping Road, with Howards Nursery on the right.

Turn left and reach a car sales area at the junction with Common Road on the left; just ahead is the Ada Cole Donkey Sanctuary. Turn left along Common Lane - Waltham Abbey road. Pass the Black Swan Inn on the right and immediately after and before the house - Merrimount - turn right, as footpath signed along a narrow fenced and hedge path. Keep straight ahead to a stile and pass the greenhouses of a nursery on the left. Cross a footbridge and keep ahead with a hedge on your right and another nursery. Reach another footbridge and turn right and left to continue and cross an open field. Basically keep to the high ground with views to your right. Reach a stile and turn right and left to continue along high ground with a fence to your left to reach a stile on the left and the churchyard of Nazeing church. Turn left through the churchyard to the road - Betts Lane.

Follow the lane past Hoe lane on the right and then the Old School House, dates 1855. Keep ahead along Betts Lane and pass the Nazeing Triangle - small nature reserve, and Back Lane. Pass the other end of the triangle and keep ahead a short distance to where the lane turns left. Here, turn right as footpath signed - Nazeing Common 0.8 km. Follow the drive towards the large white, Nazeing Park house. Nearing its entrance, keep left and follow the stiled path as you continue descending with the mansion on the right. Cross a drive and descend to a stile on the right, beside Nazeing Park Cottage; this leads to Back Lane. Turn left along the lane to the Red House and the Bumbles Green/Waltham Abbey road.

Go straight across to a permissive path sign and ascend the gate. Keep straight ahead on a track by the hedge on the right. At the end, a path on your right from Bumbles Green joins the path. *(If you walk to Bumbles Green opposite the King Harold Head Inn, turn left, as path signed. Follow the path ahead then left along the field edge to this path junction).* Turn left and soon right and start ascending soon with Copy Wood on the right. Ascend to the top with a pond and Stort Valley Way signs. Turn left along a wide grassy swathe - Epping Long Green. Soon pass three houses on the right. 1/4 mile later pass the solitary, The Cottage, on the right. Continue ahead along this former wide drove road with hedges, and a further 1/2 mile returns you to Epping Green where you began.

THREE FOREST WAY - 60 miles (96 km) with 3,081 feet (939m) of ascent. Created in 1977 by the West Essex Group of the Ramblers Association. Links together the forests of Hainault, Hatfield and Epping.

NAZEING CHURCH, dedicated to All Saints - The original Saxon settlement was in this area; a solitary church is usually a sign of a "lost" village. The village, Nasinga, is recorded in the Domesday Book, and was linked to Canons of Waltham Abbey. The name means, *"Settlers on a spur of land"*, which accounts for the views from this area. The church dates from the 12th. century with the nave. Inside is a 14th. century iron bound chest, 15th. century octagonal font, a 15th. century timber roofs and hatchments from the Palmer family of Nazeing Park. Among the memorials is one to

33

America; one of the Pilgrim father's - John Curtiss - was baptised here on September 15th. 1577.

NAZEING PARK - Built between 1780 - 1820 by William Palmer a merchant of London. Two single storey wings and a balustrated front portico. The Palmer's lived here until 1939.

Herd of fallow deer, seen as I began the ascent past Copy Wood.

Former RAF North Weald Airfield - Today's Museum and Debt of Honour memorial.

AROUND NORTH WEALD BASSETT - 6 MILES

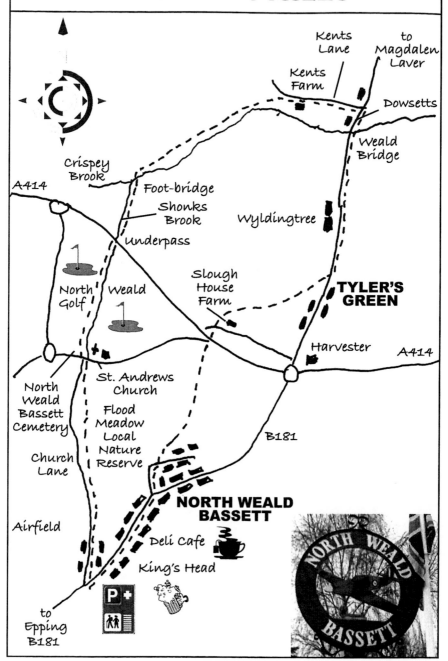

Kents Lane

to Magdalen Laver

Kents Farm

Dowsetts

Weald Bridge

Crispey Brook

A414

Foot-bridge

Shonks Brook

Wyldingtree

Underpass

Slough House Farm

TYLER'S GREEN

North Weald Golf

Harvester

A414

North Weald Bassett Cemetery

St. Andrews Church

Flood Meadow Local Nature Reserve

B181

Church Lane

NORTH WEALD BASSETT

Airfield

Deli Cafe

King's Head

to Epping B181

AROUND NORTH WEALD BASSETT
- 6 MILES
- allow 2 1/2 hours

Basic route - King's Head, North Weald Bassett - Church Lane - Flood Meadow - St. Andrew's Church - North Weald Golf Course - Cripsey Brook - Kents Farm - Weald Bridge - Wyldingtree - Tyler's Green - A414 - North Weald Bassett.

Maps - O.S. 1:25,000 Explorer Series Nos. -
- 174 - Epping Forest & Lee Valley.
- 183 - Chelmsford & The Rodings.

Car Park & Start - Roadside parking in North Weald, near the King's Head Inn and shopping area. Alternative parking area opposite St. Andrew's church or North Weald Bassett Cemetery.

Inns - King's Head, North Weald Bassett. Off the route beside the junction of the B181 and A414 is a Harvester Restaurant.

Cafe - Deli Cafe, North Weald Bassett.

ABOUT THE WALK - A pleasant short walk exploring the area to the immediate north of North Weald Bassett. First you walk across the Flood Meadow -a local Nature Reserve - to reach St. Andrew's church. Here you keep the Shonks Brook company as you cross the North Weald Golf Course to Cripsey Brook. You follow this eastwards to Weald Bridge. Now heading southwards you pass Wyldingtree Farm and onto the outskirts of Tyler's Green. Here you loop past the houses to cross the A414 to reach your final path. This leads to the edge of North Weald Bassett and your return back into the village, past the village sign, shops to the timber framed King's Head.

North Weald Airfield, which you see from the walk, has a fascinating history. Although off the route, perhaps a visit to the Museum there - open Summer months - after the walk; just down the B181 (1/3 mile) towards Epping. Plus

37

the Memorial and Debt of Honour, infront of the museum, and former entrance to the former RAF Airfield (1916 - 1964). Today the airfield is famous for its weekly car boot sale.

WALKING INSTRUCTIONS - Starting from the King's Head area in North Weald Bassett; facing the inn keep right (towards Epping) along the B181 road a few metres to Church Lane on the right. Turn right along the lane's righthand side. House No. 9 has a blue plaque - *"Margaret Rose Young 1888 - 1958 - lyricist lived here."*

Keep ahead to the end of the houses on the right and a path sign. The path is along the lefthand side of the field to a drive and large flood lake on the right. Bear right along its upper edge - a Local Nature Reserve to a gate. Cross the drive and walk along the righthand side of the field, along the Flood Meadow. To your left is the North Weald Airfield, but you get better views on your return to North Weald Bassett. Continue near the hedge to the road with St. Andrew's church opposite.

Cross the road, with access to the church on the right. Turn left a few metres to a path and sign - Bassetts Millennium Walk - Sewalds Hall. Just to your left is the North Weald Bassett Cemetery. Follow the path with the cemetery on the left and churchyard over the ditch, on the right. Continue to the North Weald Golf Course. Basically keep ahead along the edge, past the 18th tee, guided by orange marker posts. Keep Shonks Brook on your right to the A414 road. Cross the brook and walk through an underpass. Pass the 5th. tee and keep ahead, still following the orange posts. The brook is now on your left. Pass a pond on the right and reach a footbridge over Cripsey Brook and gain the signed Stort Valley Way. Turn right, westwards, and keep the brook on your right for the next 1/2 mile. As you do so cross several small footbridges. Reach Kents Lane and turn right to pass Kents Farm (Boarding Kennels) and Anvil Barn. Follow the lane to a road junction beside Dowsetts, a particularly attractive thatched house. You are on the edge of Magdalen Laver.

Turn right along the road and soon cross Weald Bridge over the Cripsey Brook. Continue along the quiet road and pass the large house, Wyldingtree on the

38

right. Soon after as approach the houses of Tyler's Green, turn right onto a track - bridlepath signed. This leads around the houses to a road, 1/4 mile away, beside Slough House Farm. Go straight across, as bridlepath signed, and follow a tarmaced path to the A414 road. Cross with care and keep ahead on a path beside the field hedge on your left. To your right can be seen the airfield. Approaching the houses of North Weald Bassett, turn right along the field edge. In 200 metres, turn left to a path sign and Queens Road. Turn right and follow the road as it curves left to reach the B181 road. Turn right and soon pass on the right the village sign with a Hurricane plane and Millennium Walk Information Board. Continue along the road past the shopping area, cafe and regain the King's Head Inn area, where you began.

KING'S HEAD INN, NORTH WEALD BASSETT - Exceptional timber framed building, believed to date back to the 15th. century and is one of the few old buildings in North Weald Bassett. Many of the buildings were destroyed during WW2.

FLOOD MEADOW - Capable of holding 38 million gallons of water to prevent flooding in North Weald. The area has more than 180 different flowers recorded. A wide variety of birds can also be spotted during the seasons.

ST. ANDREW'S CHURCH - The second church on the site and dates from 1330. Much of it is 14th. century. The high red bricked tower was built in 1500.

RAF NORTH WEALD AIRFIELD - Operational from August 1916, and within two months had successfully downed a Zeppelin at Potters Bar. The true story relates that 2nd. Lieutenant Wulstan Tempest, was eating a meal with his fiancé in Epping. He received a phone call and jumped on his motorbike to the airfield. Took off, shot the Zeppelin down and returned to airfield and back to his meal in Epping! During WW2 planes from the base destroyed more than 500 German aircraft. More than seven nations were stationed here. After the war the Black Arrows aerobatic team were stationed here. The base closed in 1964 and later sold to Epping Forest D. C. in the early 1980's.

The memorial was officially unveiled in June 1952 by the Crown Princess of Norway. The granite obelisk shows two Norwegian squadrons who were stationed here. Behind a brass door in the surrounding memorial is a Debt of Honour - a list of all who served and died here over the decades.

16th. century Istrain stone, carved with the Madonna and child, in St. Germain's church, Bobbingworth - see next walk.

CHIPPING ONGAR · GREENSTED GREEN · BOBBINGWORTH & MORETON · 10 MILES

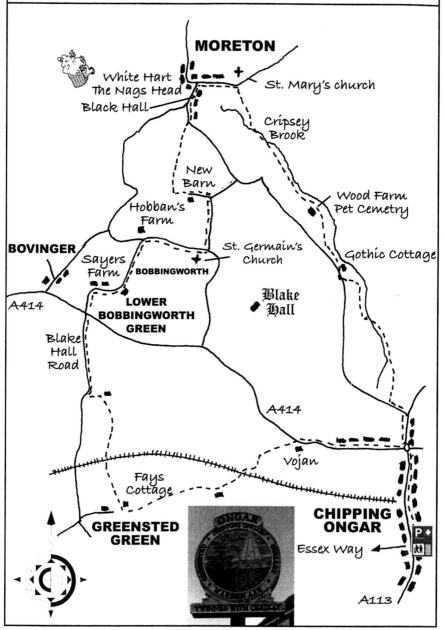

MORETON

White Hart
The Nags Head
Black Hall

St. Mary's church

Cripsey Brook

New Barn

Hobban's Farm

Wood Farm
Pet Cemetery

BOVINGER

Sayers Farm

St. Germain's Church

Gothic Cottage

BOBBINGWORTH

A414

LOWER BOBBINGWORTH GREEN

Blake Hall

Blake Hall Road

A414

Vojan

Fays Cottage

CHIPPING ONGAR

GREENSTED GREEN

Essex Way

A113

CHIPPING ONGAR, GREENSTED GREEN, BOBBINGWORTH & MORETON
- 10 MILES
- Allow 4 hours.

Basic route - Chipping Ongar Library - A414 - Greensted Green - Blake Hall Road - Lower Bobbingworth Green - Bobbingworth - New Barn - Moreton - Cripsey Brook - Wood Farm - Cripsey Brook - Chipping Ongar.

Map - O.S. 1:25,000 Explorer Series No. 183 - Chelmsford & The Rodings.

Car Park and Start - Chipping Ongar Library Car Park (Opposite Budworth Hall on A113) - Free on Saturday's and Sunday's. Limited to 2 hours weekdays. Roadside parking nearby.

Inns - The White Hart and The Nags Head, Moreton. The Two Brewers, Royal Oak in Chipping Ongar, off the route at the end.

Cafe - Several in Chipping Ongar.

ABOUT THE WALK - A delightful mixture of paths and single track roads lead you to Bobbingworth and it's hidden gem, St. Germain's church. Closeby is Blake Hall and a possible extension to visit the gardens. More than a mile later you reach the Conservation area of Moreton, with inns, old hall and church; more than halfway! You return to Chipping Ongar beside Cripsey Brook, on the way passing a pet cemetery. A rewarding walk in unspoilt countryside. I walked this at the end of January with a dusting of snow on the ground. I saw no other walkers, just blue tits, long tailed tits, wrens, robins, jays, crows a white egret and a few snowdrops just coming into flower.

WALKING INSTRUCTIONS - From Chipping Ongar Library, opposite Budworth Hall, turn right along the main road (A113) to the main roundabout (A414) road beside a BP Garage, passing Great Stony Park on the right and Bowes House on the lefthand corner; - you will return to here at the end, along Fyfield Road. Turn left along the A414 Harlow Road for 1/2 mile, along the righthand side (pavement) to Vojan Restaurant. Before it on the left is an old milepost - London 22 miles; Epping 6 miles; Ongar 1 mile. Turn left at the restaurant onto a track - path signed, New Barns 1/2 mile. Follow the hedged path, which soon swings left and right to cross a bridge over the railway line - Epping - Ongar line. Soon after reach woodland and a solitary house on the left. Keep ahead, now on a path in woodland and follow it for 1/2 mile to the start of a road and Fay's Cottage on the right.

Immediately after the cottage, turn right, as path signed, along a fenced path to an open field. The path line is faint here, but aim slightly left to the right of large barns and a few trees on the right, and ditch, and descend slightly to reach a stile and railway line. Cross to another stile and field. Turn right and left, as path arrowed, to walk down the righthand field edge past pine trees on the right. Later the path becomes a track past more woodland to a solitary house. Follow the drive left to Blake Hall Road. Turn right and follow the road to the A414 road. Cross into the lane and enter Lower Bobbingworth Green. Follow the road right past Sayers Farm, and continue along the single tracked road as it curves left, ascending gently to a road junction near Hobban's Farm. As you walked to your right you will have seen the tower of St. Germain's church; your destination.

Turn right to reach the hamlet of Bobbingworth with the School House dated 1856 and St. Germain's Church on the right. Further along the road is the entrance to Blake Hall. Just after the church turn left along Gainsthorpe Road. In 1/4 mile it turns right, turn left here along Newhouse Lane. Pass New Barn and keep straight ahead on a Public Byway. Soon after turn right, at a path post and follow a path along the field edge and by a hedge on the right. Reach a footbridge and turn right and left and reach the road on the outskirts of Moreton and Conservation Area.

Turn left along the road crossing Moreton Bridge over Cripsey Brook. Soon after on your right, as you ascend, is Black Hall. Just after reach a junction with the Nags Head infront and the White Hart on the left. Turn right to pass and soon bear slightly left onto a path to St. Mary's church. After visiting turn right to the road, and right along it to Hancock's house with the Old Rectory on the right. Turn left through a squeeze stile and descend gently, leftwards, to the Cripsey Brook and follow it to a metal footbridge. Cross and turn left, first with a hedge on your left then open fields, following a defined path with the brook well to your left. Reach two stiles as the brook return to you on the left, as you approach Wood Farm. Follow the stiles and signs well to the left of the farm and reach a Pet Cemetery (Cats and Dogs) on the right - well worth a visit.

Continue past the edge of it to a small footbridge and onto another near the Moreton road. Keep near it to a stile by a solitary oak tree and gain the road. Turn left and pass Gothic Cottage and soon after left at a stile and path sign. Cross the field towards the brook but as signed turn right keeping the brook to your left to reach another metal footbridge. Cross and aim for a kissing gate halfway up the righthand side of the field. Through, continue on a defined path across the grassy field to the outskirts of Chipping Ongar and Moreton Road. Turn left to the main road - Fyfield Road, Ongar 1 mile. Turn right and soon reach the BP Petrol Station. Cross the righthand side of the roundabout, passing Bowes House, and retrace your steps back along the A113 to Chipping Ongar Library.

St. Germain's church, Bobbingworth.

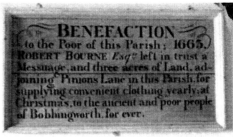

Font and Benefactor's notice, St. Germain's church, Bobbingworth.

ST. GERMAIN'S CHURCH, BOBBINGWORTH - The plain outside gives no hint of the splendour within; it is a little gem. Bobbingworth, a Saxon name, means "The place of Oxen". Parts of the church date back to the 13th. century. Near the doorway can be seen a 16th. century block of Istrain stone, carved with the Madonna and child. Belonged to the Capel Cure family, who reside at Blake Hall, it has been used as a memorial to Major George Capel-Cure and his wife, Ione. Infront of it is the 15th. century font; the top was found in Little Pardon churchyard and returned to its base, many years ago. The font once had a locked cover to prevent witches from taking the Holy water. There are many monuments to the Capel Cure family inside the church and outside on a small mound in the churchyard is the sad table top memorial to Elizabeth Cure, the first wife of Capel Cure of Blake Hall who died on November 2nd. 1773, aged 21. On the otherside is Joanna Cure 2nd wife of Capel Cure who died June 3rd. 1804, aged 43. On a side panel is recorded, Capel Cure died January 21st. 1820, aged 70.

St. Germain (Germanus of Auxere) born in 378 AD and died in Italy, 448 AD. A French hunter and Chieftain who had the Bishopric of Auxere thrust upon him. He helped Briton's to form an army whose battle cry was, Alleluia, and defeated the Picts in North Wales. He visited this area of England as a missionary

46

BLAKE HALL - Bought by the Capel Cure family in 1789. The gardens are regularly opened to the public during the summer. The building is mostly 18th. century but includes part of the earlier 17th. century building.

Black Hall, Moreton.

MORETON - The central part is a Conservation Area, with the Black Hall, the oldest building. Formerly a Guildhall Cottage where the Guild of All Saints, founded in 1473, met. The Nag's Head Inn (formerly know as the Moreton Massey Public House), is 16th. century and originally two cottages. The White Hart also dates back to 16th. century.

St, Mary's church, Moreton - inside and out. Contains medieval wall paintings.

Pet Cemetery at Wood Farm.

Ongar 1 mile; milepost beside the A414 road.

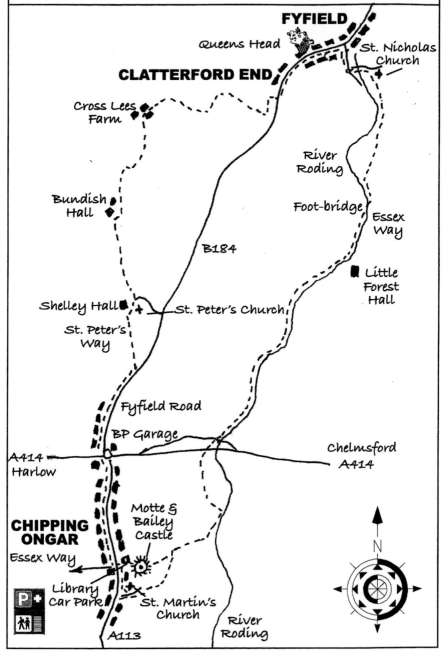

CHIPPING ONGAR AND FYFIELD - 8 MILES

FYFIELD

Queens Head

St. Nicholas Church

CLATTERFORD END

Cross Lees Farm

River Roding

Foot-bridge

Essex Way

Bundish Hall

B184

Little Forest Hall

Shelley Hall

St. Peter's Church

St. Peter's Way

Fyfield Road

BP Garage

A414 Harlow

Chelmsford A414

CHIPPING ONGAR

Motte & Bailey Castle

Essex Way

Library Car Park

St. Martin's Church

River Roding

A113

N

CHIPPING ONGAR
AND FYFIELD
- 8 MILES
- allow 3 1/2 hours

Basic route - Chipping Ongar (Library) - A113 - Fyfield Road - St. Peter's Way - Shelley Hall - St. Peter's church - Bundish Hall - Cross Lees Farm - Clatterford End - Fyfield - St. Nicholas Church - River Roding - Essex Way - A414 - Motte & Bailey Castle - St. Martin's Church - Chipping Ongar.

Map - O.S. 1:25,000 Explorer Series Nos. - 183 - Chelmsford & The Rodings.

Car Park & Start - Chipping Ongar Library Car Park - opposite Budworth Hall on the A113. Free on Saturday's and Sunday's.

Inns - Queens Head, Fyfield. The Cock Tavern, Chipping Ongar.

Cafe - Chipping Ongar.

ABOUT THE WALK - A beautiful quiet walk, through enjoyable scenery. After leaving Chipping Ongar you pick up a section of St. Peter's Way to Shelley Hall and St. Peter's church. From here you follow a bridleway to Cross Lees farm and then on along good signed paths to Clatterford End. Just after you reach the attractive unspoilt village of Fyfield with the Queens Head Inn, basically halfway! The village is among the best kept in the area and has won and been runner up in past years. The River Roding is particularly attractive here and you have a beautiful view of it from a bridge. You follow the gentle river southwards, but before doing so a visit to the ancient St. Nicholas church, is most worthwhile. The river path is also part of the Essex Way and brings back to Chipping Ongar, some three miles away. As you near the village you pick up again part of the St. Peter's Way. You also have the choice of going more direct into Chipping Ongar via the Motte & Bailey Castle to the Library car park, or via the historical route to St. Martin's church and Wren House.

51

WALKING INSTRUCTIONS - Starting from the Library car park, turn right along the main road - A113. Follow it for more than 1/2 mile to the roundabout with the A414 and BP Garage beyond. Walk around the righthand side to reach the B184 Fyfield road. Soon pass Moreton Road and the Smith Brassiere on the left. Pass the 30 mph sign and turn left along a drive; footpath signed, beside the thatched Shelley Lodge. The drive is part of St. Peter's Way. Approaching Shelley Hall, turn right before the entrance gateposts to reach St. Peter's church. Walk past the lefthand side of the church to entrance gate and track. Turn right and in a few metres left, along a bridlepath signed track. This soon turns left and on the corner keep straight ahead, as signed by a footpath post, and follow the defined path along the field edge to Bundish Hall, 1/2 mile away.

Reaching the drive, turn right with a well defined moat on your left. Soon after turn left, as bridlepath signed, along the drive. Pass Bundish Hall on the left, as the bridleway becomes a grass track. Later keep a hedge on your left as the track turns right and left, becoming a hedged grass track. Again, later there is just a hedge on your left as you follow the grass track to Cross Lees Farm. Turn right immediately before the building along the field edge, passing the building on your left. Just after reach a path post. The defined path crosses the middle of the field and turns right, now a track. This whole route from Cross Lees Farm to Clatterford End - about 3/4 mile - is well marked with yellow arrow posts. The track becomes a path for awhile with a hedge on the left to another marker post. Turn left, as indicated, still with a hedge on your left. Reach another path post and turn right, heading for houses. Before them turn left and soon right to reach the road (B194) at Clatterford End. Turn left for Fyfield.

Follow the road into the village to the Post Office, Shop and Queens Head Inn. Turn right to pass the School House on the left and the Missionary House on the right - Former Free Church dated 1904. Soon after bear left across a bridge with a magnificent view of the River Rodin and Riverside and Mill Lodge. Continue towards St. Nicholas church, before it turn right, as path signed. The church is well worth a visit.

You are now on the Essex Way with the river on your right. Soon on your left are pine trees. Continue on the path to a path marker post and cross an open field to a footbridge across the river. Cross and turn left, still on the Essex Way and for the next 2 miles the river is on your left. Cross several small footbridges and pass Little Forest Hall to your left. Continue near the river on your left and in 1/2 mile reach woodland on either side of you. Here you cross three bridges in quick succession and then another with a stile. Continue on the path near the river to a stile and side road. Cross to another stile and reach the A414 road, Cross with care to another stile and steps. Walk past a wood on your left and soon after turn left on the defined path to a footbridge over the River Rodin, and now back on St. Peter's Way.

Don't cross the bridge, but turn right along the banks of the river, with woodland on your left. In a short distance turn right and ascend slightly with a hedge on your right. At the top reach a squeeze stile. Turn left and pass a skate park and children's play area. Here, as signed you turn right onto a path to the Motte & Bailey Castle and onto Chipping Ongar Library car park. To visit St. Martins church and historical Chipping Ongar, Continue on the path to a house. Turn left and right, as path signed and follow the path, which is part of St. Peter's Way. Look for a turning on the right to St. Martin's Church. After your visit descend past the Wren House to the main street and turn right to regain the Library car park.

ST. PETER'S WAY - 41 miles/66 km. Starts from Chipping Ongar, Essex (TI552029) and ends at St. Peter's Flat, Essex (TM031082). The walk's logo are crossed keys on a red background.

ST. PETER'S CHURCH, SHELLEY - Third church on the site, built in 1888. On the right of the entrance can be seen 18th. century gravestone; older than the church. You will also note the untouched area near the entrance. Beneath the ground is a pit where the plague victims were buried in the 14th. century. The churchyard is open; no walls. Shelley is mentioned in the Domesday Book - Senleia; could well be a lost village site.

53

FYFIELD - Best kept village in Essex in 2008; runner up in 2007 and 2009. Mentioned in the Domesday Book. In the 14th. century owned by the Scrope family. Henry le Scrope was tried for treason and beheaded; his head is said to buried under the present organ in the church.

ST. NICHOLAS CHURCH - Dates back to the 12th. century with central tower. The nave is 12th century. Fragments of roman brick can be seen in the base of the tower and nave. The chancel was built in 1330. The Purbeck marble font is 12th. century.

CHIPPING ONGAR -

MOTTE & BAILEY - Norman with well defined motte and banks. Never rebuilt in stone and its "life" lasted little more than a century.

ST. MARTIN'S CHURCH - Norman and medieval workmanship. The tower is 15th. century. The 15th. century font sits on a new base; the font was found in someone's garden in 1963! The oak pulpit is 16th. century. The chancel roof dates from 1647, inscribed on the central king post. The two scissors beams are believed to be original and dates from the 11th. century. In the chancel on the left of the altar is a small wooden window door. Behind is rare anchorite cell and the hermit could watch the service from here. St.

Martin (317-397 AD) became a monk when aged 40 and later became Bishop of Tours.

Outside doorway to the Anchorite Cell.

Wren House and passageway to St. Martin's Church.

WREN HOUSE - 18th. century timber framed house, with original shop window. The timber framed building opposite has a doorway dated 1642.

BUDWORTH HALL - Built in 1886 in memory of Capt. Budworth of Greensted Hall, as an assembly room, reading room for the "young men of the town".

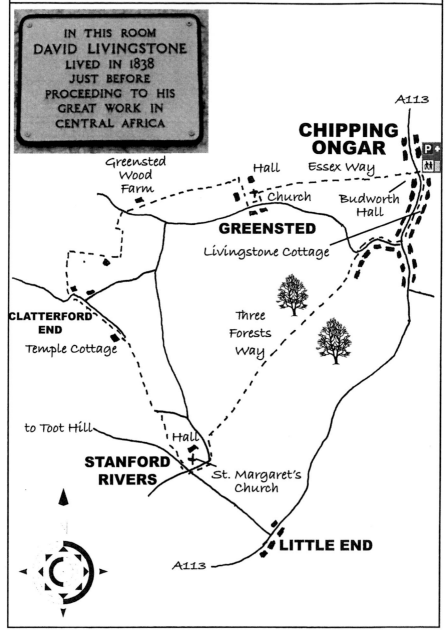

IN THIS ROOM
DAVID LIVINGSTONE
LIVED IN 1838
JUST BEFORE
PROCEEDING TO HIS
GREAT WORK IN
CENTRAL AFRICA

A113

CHIPPING ONGAR

Hall   Essex Way

Greensted Wood Farm

Church

Budworth Hall

GREENSTED

Livingstone Cottage

CLATTERFORD END

Temple Cottage

Three Forests Way

to Toot Hill

Hall

STANFORD RIVERS

St. Margaret's Church

LITTLE END

A113

CHIPPING ONGAR, GREENSTED, CLATTERFORD END, & STANFORD RIVERS
- 6 MILES
- Allow 3 hours.

Basic route - Chipping Ongar Library - Essex Way - Greensted Church - Greensted Wood Farm - Clatterford End - Temple Cottage - Stanford Rivers - Three Forest Way - Chipping Ongar.

Map - O.S. 1:25,000 Explorer Series No. 183 - Chelmsford & The Rodings.

Car Park and Start - Chipping Ongar Library Car Park (Opposite Budworth Hall on A113) - Free on Saturday's and Sunday's. Limited to 2 hours weekdays. Roadside parking nearby.

Inns - The Two Brewers, Royal Oak in Chipping Ongar.

Cafe - Several in Chipping Ongar.

ABOUT THE WALK - Gentle rolling countryside to the west of Chipping Ongar. You follow sections of the Essex Way and Three Forests Way. You pass three hamlets - Greensted, Clatterford End and Stanford Rivers, as you do so you see the Saxon Greensted church and the Norman church of St. Margaret's at Stanford Rivers. Once you leave Chipping Ongar there are no facilities until you return there. The whole route is along defined paths and quiet lanes.

WALKING INSTRUCTIONS - Opposite Chipping Ongar Library, turn left past Budworth Hall and Sainsbury's, descending to a track and the Essex Way; heading due west. Keep straight ahead for more than 1/2 mile to a footbridge, trees and drive. Cross over to a fenced path and continue ahead to the next drive - to Greensted Hall - and turn left past Church Lodge to the road in the hamlet of Greensted. On your right is the wooden Saxon church.

Turn right along the road, as path signed - New Barns 1/2 mile (Ongar 1 mile). Pass The Granary (wooden building) on the right and follow the track beyond for 40 meters to a footpath sign, still on the Essex Way, on your left. The defined path is at first a fenced and hedged one. Later you keep the hedge on your right. Soon after cross a footbridge and keep ahead with woodland on the right, passing Greensted Wood Farm on the right, before reaching a road.

Turn left and right to continue on the signed Essex Way. Soon reach a kissing gate and turn left and right again to gently ascend through four squeeze stiles, with woodland on your right, passing scaffolding field boundaries on the left, to a kissing gate. Turn right on the defined path and pass a solitary house on the left. Soon after look for a small metal gate on the left. Leave the Essex Way here, and follow the path through woodland to another gate. Turn right and soon after at the end of the woodland on the right and wooden fence, turn left along a track to a wooden path post and trees. Bear slightly left along the path beside the field edge to reach the houses of Clatterford End, opposite Fairdene. Turn right along the road to a junction and turn left along Colemans Lane - No Through Road.

Pass Colemans Farm and Temple Cottage and keep ahead on a path (byway), which is hedged and lined with trees. It was along here that six fallow deer suddenly crossed the path infront of me; one of the delights of quiet walking! The path becomes more of a track and curves left, as it does so take the second right of way on the right, signed. Cross the field to its top righthand corner and stile. Turn left over it along the edge to another two stiles and the road in Stanford Rivers. Turn left, passing the hall on the left and reach St. Margaret's Church.

Just after turn left along Mutton Row, passing the otherside of the church and farm on left. Follow the road left to Ambermead and turn right, as footpath signed onto a track. You are now on the Three Forests Way. For more than a mile you keep straight ahead on the track, passing woodland on the your right and left to reach the outskirts of Chipping Ongar. Continue ahead on a path then onto a road, past a school and children's play area to gain Greensted Road. Turn right to reach the A113 and The Two Brewers Inn. Turn left to walk through the shopping area of Chipping Ongar, passing the Royal Oak and Livingstone Cottage on the right. Soon after reach Budworth Hall and Chipping Ongar Library.

GREENSTED CHURCH, DEDICATED TO ST. ANDREW - A very rare building which rightly claims to be the oldest wooden church in the world and the oldest wooden building standing in Europe. Dates from Saxon times with 51 vertical oak logs. Close to the porch is a Crusader's grave. Above the logs is a Tudor tiled roof with Victorian windows. The timber tower has weatherboard cladding. In the chancel is a stained glass winder to St. Andrew, the brother St. Peter. Opposite is one to St. Edmund who was martyred in 869 AD and was, for awhile, the patron saint of England. His main shrine is at Bury St. Albans. For awhile his body was kept in London and 1013 was returned to Bury St. Edmunds, and enroute was rested here at Greensted. A beam records the legend of his martyrdom.

ST. MARGARET'S CHURCH, STANFORD RIVERS. Norman with five narrow Norman widows, and dates from 1150 AD.

Stanford Rivers church,
dedicated to St. Margaret.
and brass, dated 1584.

THESE COTTAGES ARE VESTED IN
TRUSTEES FOR THE BENEFIT OF
ONGAR CONGREGATIONAL CHURCH
PURSUANT TO THE WISHES OF
THE LATE JOSIAH GILBERT
IN MEMORIAM AUGUST 15ᵗʰ 1892.

IN THIS ROOM
DAVID LIVINGSTONE
LIVED IN 1838
JUST BEFORE
PROCEEDING TO HIS
GREAT WORK IN
CENTRAL AFRICA

Livingstone Cottages,
Chipping Ongar.

TOOT HILL, LOG CHURCH & CHIPPING ONGAR - 6 MILES

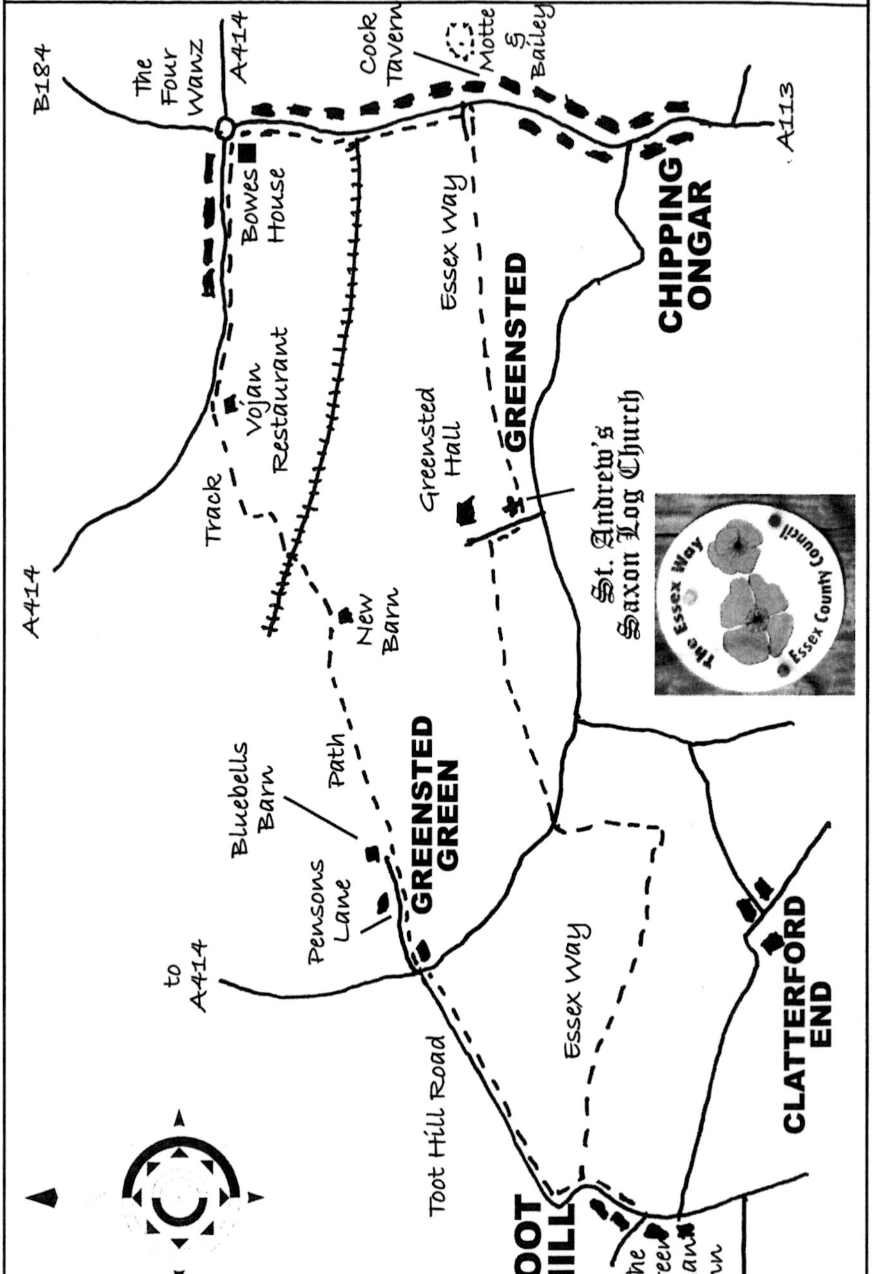

B184

The Four Wanz

A414

Cock Tavern

Motte & Bailey

A113

CHIPPING ONGAR

Bowes House

Essex Way

GREENSTED

Vojan Restaurant

Track

A414

Greensted Hall

St. Andrew's Saxon Log Church

The Essex Way

Essex County Council

New Barn

Path

Bluebells Barn

GREENSTED GREEN

Pensons Lane

to A414

Essex Way

CLATTERFORD END

Toot Hill Road

TOOT HILL

The Green Man Inn

62

TOOT HILL,
LOG CHURCH
& CHIPPING ONGAR
- 6 MILES
- allow 3 hours.

Basic route - Toot Hill - Essex Way - Greensted Farm - Greensted - St. Andrew's (Log Church) - Essex Way - Chipping Ongar - A414 - New Barns - Greensted Green - Toot Hill.

Map - O.S. 1:25,000 Explorer Series No. 183 - Chelmsford & The Rodings.

Car Park & Start - Limited roadside parking in Toot Hill beside the green (Barnmead) Grid Ref. 515025. Just north of the Green Man Inn.

Inns - Green Man Inn, Toot Hill. The Cock Tavern, Chipping Ongar. Others in Chipping Ongar off the route.

Cafe - Chipping Ongar - off the route in main part of the village.

ABOUT THE WALK - The highlight of this walk is the truly amazing Saxon Log Church at Greensted. I have chosen to start from Toot Hill, on purpose, for a building like this needs to be walked to and earnt to see. Toot Hill has a fine inn with the best Green Man inn sign I have seen. After the Log Church you continue along the Essex Way to Chipping Ongar. On this walk you miss the historic centre of the village - the previous walks do this - as you head north and then west to return to Toot Hill. You follow good paths and a lane to get there. This is one walk to really relish and stop and admire the work of Saxon man to make such a delightful building tucked away in the quiet countryside of Essex. I am sure it will be a place you will return to again, and again.

WALKING INSTRUCTIONS - From Barnmead, by the green in Toot Hill, just north of Green Man inn, head northwards along Toot Hill Road, past the

63

houses on the right to the first lefthand bend. Turn right, as path signed, and pass Weald Lodge and join the clearly signed Essex Way, which is your path to the Log Church and Chipping Ongar. The defined path soon turns right over a footbridge and then left along a hedged path. Keep straight ahead as the path now keeps to the edge of the fields, using a footbridge. Later keep the hedge on your left and nearly 3/4 mile (15 mins) from the road in Toot Hill pass a solitary house on your right. Shortly afterwards turn left through a kissing gate and continue along the lefthand side of the field with woodland, using several squeeze stiles. Pass houses on the right and reach a kissing gate and then the Greensted road.

Cross over to a footbridge and path sign. Continue along the lefthand side of the field, with a ditch on your left, and pass Greensted Farm and woodland on your left. Ahead can be seen the white wooden church tower of the Log Church, your destination. Reach another footbridge and continue ahead still on the Essex Way, and along the field edge to a track. Turn right along it into the hamlet of Greensted. Turn left at the junction and on your left is the Log Church. After your visit continue a few metres more and turn left, as path signed, along the drive to Greensted Hall. Turn right after a few metres to continue along the Essex Way. The defined path keeps to the field edge, straight ahead, all the way to Chipping Ongar nearly a mile away. Cross a footbridge and later as you approach the village gain a track, which becomes a road as you enter the village with Sainsbury's and Budworth Hall on the right and car park on the left.

Reaching the main road, with the Library opposite and the Cock Tavern to your right, turn left. (The main part of the village is to your right.) Follow the road, northwards out of the village past houses to the crossroads at The Four Wanz and junction of the A414 - Harlow - Chelmsford Road. Turn left along the A414 righthand side, with Bowes House on the left. Follow the pavement for 1/2 mile to the end of the houses to Vojan Restaurant on the left. Cross the road to the righthand side of it to a footpath sign - New Barn 1/2 mile. Follow the hedged track, which crosses the railway line and in 1/2 mile reach New Barn house on the left and woodland. Keep straight ahead now on a path through the woodland and on along the path through a wooded strip to a house, track and enter Greensted Green. Follow the track/lane - Pensons Lane - past Bluebells Barn to the road junction.

Cross to Toot Hill Road to Toot Hill, Pass large ponds on the left at the start and follow the quiet narrow road for 3/4 mile all the way back to Toot Hill and the Green Man Inn.

ESSEX WAY - 81 miles - from Epping Station to Harwich Old Lighthouse; generally walked in ten stages. Epping Station to Chipping Ongar being Stage One. www.essexway.org.uk

GREEN MAN - The colour green means awakenings and new beginnings. The Celtic Green Man is a vegetation and fertility God. He is usually shown surrounded by oak leaves and foliage.

SAXON LOG CHURCH - Oldest wooden church in the world, dating back to 850 AD; also oldest wooden building in Europe. Located in the small hamlet of Greensted. Photo shows the rear with logs clearly visible.

CHIPPING ONGAR - Small market town with its charter being granted in the 12th. century. Weekly market - Wednesday. Remains of a Norman castle - Motte & Bailey.

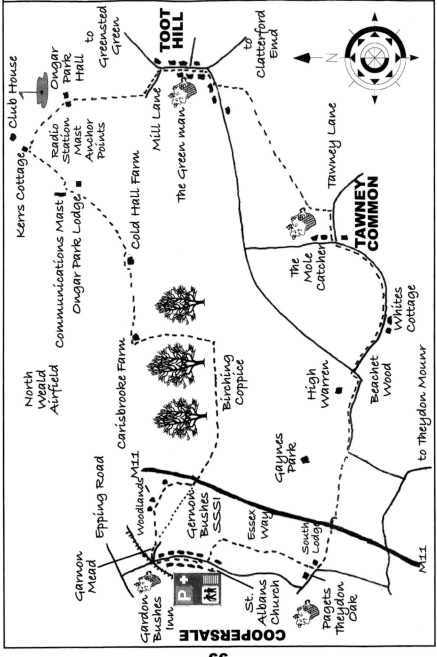

COOPERSALE (EPPING) & ONGAR PARK - 10 MILES

TOOT HILL

to Greensted Green

to Clatterford End

Club House

Ongar Park Hall

Kerrs Cottage

Radio Station Mast Anchor Points

Communications Mast

Ongar Park Lodge

Cold Hall Farm

Mill Lane

The Green Man

Tawney Lane

TAWNEY COMMON

The Mole Catcher

North Weald Airfield

Carisbrooke Farm

Birching Coppice

Whites Cottage

High Warren

Beachet Wood

to Theydon Mount

Epping Road

Woodlands

M11

Gernon Bushes SSSI

Essex Way

Gaynes Park

South Lodge

M11

Garnon Mead

Garnon Bushes Inn

P

St. Albans Church

Pagets Theydon Oak

COOPERSALE

COOPERSALE (EPPING) & ONGAR PARK
- 10 MILES
- allow 4 hours

Basic route - Coopersale,Epping - Gernon Bushes SSSI - M11 - Birching Coppice - Essex Way - Carisbrooke Farm - Cold Hall Farm - Communications Mast - Ongar Park Lodge - Golf Course - Ongar Park Hall - Toot Hill - Tawney Common - Beachet Wood - Gaynes Park - Coopersale Street - Essex Way - Coopersale.

Maps - O.S. 1:25,000 Explorer Series Nos.
- 174 - Epping Forest & Lee Valley.
- 183 - Chelmsford & The Rodings.

Car Park & Start - Limited roadside parking in Coopersale (Epping) or in Garnon Mead road. 1/4 mile off the B181 - Epping North Weald Bassett road. Grid Ref. 476032.

Inns - The Green Man Inn, Toot Hill. The Mole Trap, Tawney Common. Pagets Theydon Oak, Coopersale Street, just off the route. Garnon Bushes Inn, Coopersale.

Cafe - Nearest in Epping a mile away.

ABOUT THE WALK - The first half, since you are close to to the former RAF Airfield at North Weald, has an wartime aviation feel. First you pass the site where four bombs fell during WW2 and soon after is where a fighter plane crashed. Later you cross high ground with extensive views and pass the location and concrete anchors where many barrage balloons were secured to deter enemy planes. The second half is through the oldest deer park in England - Ongar Park, before reaching Toot Hill and the Green Man Inn. Pleasant paths lead you to the hamlet of Tawney Common, a quite little haven, with pond, seat and The Mole Trap Inn. Quiet road walking brings you past woodland to Gaynes Park, where deer roam. Soon after you rejoin the Essex Way and return to Coopersale.

WALKING INSTRUCTIONS - Starting from the Garnon Bushes Inn, turn left and right and walk along Garnon Mead. In a short distance on the left is the gate, bridlepath sign, drive/track, and entry point into Garnon Bushes SSSI. Turn left along the drive. *(You can keep straight ahead along the road, then track to the footbridge over the M11; both routes meet here.)* In less than 1/4 mile pass your first house on the left and soon after approach Woodlands. Here on the left is a small area, which in spring is full of daffodil's. This is where a bomb fell, on December 28th. 1940, and in the Woodlands the family survived by hiding in a cupboard. Continue along the track to near the M11 and a large barn. Here a fighter plane crashed on July 24th. 1940. Follow the curving track right to steps and the footbridge over the M11, on the left, - to your right is the direct, straight path from Garnon Mead.

Cross the footbridge and continue on the track/path passing woodland on the right. Later follow the path left and right to enter woodland - Birching Coppice; you are on part of the Essex Way. This 1/2 mile long straight track leads through woodland - Birching Coppice - and nearing its end walk through a grove of silver birch trees to a track junction. Here you leave the Essex Way. Turn left along the track - public byway (red arrow), in woodland, for almost 1/2 mile to Carisbrook Farm. Walk around the buildings and keep right along the drive past Cold Hill Lodge. Nearing Cold Hall Farm keep left past it, as bridlepath signed. You can see your initial destination, the prominent Communications mast. Keep a hedge on right to reach a ladder stile. Follow the path by the hedge left and pass Ongar Park Lodge. the field on the left has concrete bases in circles where the masts were secured to - you see many more over the next mile. Pass the mast on the left and on the right are extensive views eastwards. Keep ahead along the drive and cross the bridge over the Epping-Chipping Ongar railway line.

Soon after reach the road junction, with deserted buildings to the left and drive towards Ongar Park Hall. Turn right and left to a stile and path sign. Cross the field aiming for the Golf Course Club House. On the way pass more ariel mast bases of varying types, to a stile. Cross to another before Kerrs Cottage; beyond is the golf course and club house. Over the stile turn right, past the cottage to a gate and onto another, now on a bridleway. Keep the fence on your left as you walk along the field edge with more anchor points in the field on the left. Enter Ongar Park Hall and follow the drive right and pass under the railway line. Follow the drive for more than 1/4 mile to Clunes House. Turn left and now along Mill Lane follow it into Toot Hill. At the main road turn right and pass the Green Man Inn. Soon after reach the grassy triangle and village sign. Keep right along Epping road, for a few metres to a footpath sign and stile on the left. Pass golf links and follow the well stiled path, to a stile and footbridge. Cross and continue to two stiles and cross a fenced track. Continue to another stile and bear right to a path marker post and public byway.

Turn left and right to continue on the path, as you cross three open fields, and across two footbridges. After, keep the stream/ditch on your left as you walk along the field edge to your third footbridge on the left. Cross and ascend the field to a path sign and Tawney Lane. Turn right and soon reach Tawney Common with The Mole Trap Inn to the right. Turn left along the road, with a pond and seat on your left at the start. Follow the single laned road past Whites Cottage and Beachet Wood on the left to a road junction. Turn left and follow the road - Banks Lane - right past pine trees and High Warren. Pass the road turning for Theydon Mount, and keep ahead to where the road turns sharp left. On the right is the entrance to Gaynes Park. Go straight across to a gate and path sign - Coopersale Street. Walk with the hedge on your right, along a grassy strip, with views over the park on the right - perhaps seeing some deer. At the end turn right and left to cross the road bridge over the M11, to Gaynes Park. Immediately after turn left and right to continue on a path by the hedge, with the drive beyond, to a footbridge and onto the road beside South Lodge. Just ahead is the Paget's Theydon Oak Inn.

Walk ahead a few metres and turn right, as path signed, and rejoin the Essex Way. At first a hedged path and then along the lefthand side of the fields near the hedge. You gently ascend for 1/2 mile; turning left and right, and reach the woodland of Gernon Bushes by a seat - exceptional views southwards from here. Enter the wood and turn left, still on the Essex Way, to a gate at the wood's entrance. Bear left to gain the main road with St. Albans church to the left. Turn right, and walk through Coopersale, past the shops to the Garnon Bushes Inn, where you began.

GARNON BUSHES - On December 28th 1940, a lone German bomber dropped eight high explosive bombs. Four fell on North Weald airfield, one near the railway line. Another fell on the barn close to the Woodlands, damaging the building. The family hid in a cupboard and survived. Another fell closeby damaging the water main. The eighth one fell on the common. There are no bomb craters but the craters you see here were made from digging for clay and stone materials. The daffodil patch is in memory of those of the village who died during WW2.

On July 24th. 1940 Pilot Officer Jack Royston Hamar DFC and another took off to intercept a bomber over Ipswich. The bomber turned out to be a friendly Anson plane and they returned. Hamar struggled in low cloud at 100 feet and miscalculated his route and crashed here at Little Park Farm (Barn today). He came from Knighton in Radnorshire, Wales, and is buried there.

Garnon Bushes SSSI - A variety of flora and fauna can be seen, including ragged robin. There are grass snakes but you are more likely to see Slow Worms.

Essex Way signs - old and new - as seen on the walk.

RADIO STATION MAST BASES - There were many radio masts in the area, secured to a variety of bases, between 1920 -1980, many built by the Marconi Company, reaching a height of 300 feet. Some of the Radio Station buildings still remain, and you passed close to them on the left, on the summit of the high ground. The site is a former fort, known as The Redoubt, erected in 1889 for the defence of London from a Prussian invasion, that never happend.

ONGAR PARK - First deer park in England dating back to the mid 11th. century.

The Mole Trap Inn, Tawney Common.

GAYNES PARK - Built in the 19th. century. The barn is now a popular wedding venue.

COOPERSALE - St. Albans church built in 1852 at the bequest of Miss Archer-Houblon. Garnon Bushes inn made from a row of cottages.

Snowdrops in the churchyard of Theydon Garnon All Saints church.

Footbridge over the River Roding, near Patch Park - see next walk.

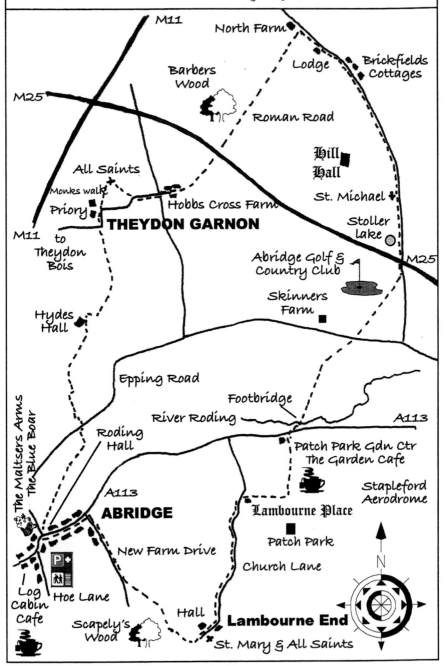

ABRIDGE, THEYDON GARNON & HILL HALL - 9 1/2 MILES

M11

North Farm

Lodge

Brickfields Cottages

Barbers Wood

M25

Roman Road

Hill Hall

All Saints

St. Michael

Monks walk

Priory

Hobbs Cross Farm

THEYDON GARNON

Stoller lake

M11

to Theydon Bois

Abridge Golf & Country Club

M25

Skinners Farm

Hydes Hall

Epping Road

Footbridge

River Roding

A113

The Maltsers Arms
The Blue Boar

Roding Hall

Patch Park Gdn Ctr
The Garden Cafe

A113

Stapleford Aerodrome

ABRIDGE

Lambourne Place

Patch Park

New Farm Drive

Church Lane

N

Log Cabin Cafe

Hoe Lane

Hall

Lambourne End

Scapely's Wood

St. Mary & All Saints

ABRIDGE, THEYDON GARNON & HILL HALL
- 9 1/2 MILES
- allow 4 hours.

Basic route - Abridge - River Roding - Hydes Hall - All Saints Church, Theydon Garnon - Hobbs Cross Farm - M25 - Roman Road - North Farm - Theydon Mount - Hill Hall - St. Michael Church - M25 - River Roding - Patch Park - Lambourne House - St. Mary & All Saints church, Lambourne End - Abridge.

Map - O.S. 1:25,000 Explorer Series No. 174 - Epping Forest & Lee Valley.

Car Park and Start - Limited roadside parking in Hoe Lane, opposite the Maltsers Arms in Abridge.

Inns - The Maltsers Arms and The Blue Boar, Abridge.

Cafe - The Log Cabin, Abridge. The Garden Cafe, Patch Park Garden Centre.

ABOUT THE WALK - All on well defined paths and lanes. First you head northwards from Abridge to pass Hydes Hall to reach Theydon Garnon and its historical church. Soon after you pass Hobbs Cross Farm, pass under the M25 and follow the line of a Roman Road to North Farm. Here you follow a quiet road past the historic Hill House and St. Michael's church before crossing the M25. Afterwards you follow a path to the a footbridge over the River Roding with Stapleford Aerodrome nearby. You pass a garden centre and cafe and reach Lambourne House. From here you walk along the quiet Church Lane to Lambourne End and the wooden St. Mary & All Saints church. A short path returns you to Abridge, after a fascinating circuit.

WALKING INSTRUCTIONS - Starting from Hoe Lane return to main road and turn right and pass The Blue Boar Inn on the left. Shortly afterwards turn left along the B172 Abridge road, and pass Roding Hall on the right. Cross the bridge over the River Roding and turn right, as path signed. Walk along the righthand field edge near the river to a stile. Continue near the river and aim for the far lefthand corner of the field, where there is a stile. Turn left keeping the hedge on your right to reach a lane. Turn right and left, as path signed. Keep the hedge on your left for a few metres before turning left and right, now with the hedge and ditch on your right. Continue to a footbridge on your right. Cross and turn left keeping the hedge and ditch on your left. Continue to a stile and footpath sign. Here, the rights of way fork. Bear half right up the middle of the field, aiming for the righthand side of Hydes Hall. Over the brow of the field you can see the stile you are aiming for. Over, gain the drive and keep straight ahead along it past the hall on the left. Follow the drive right to a path sign on the left; behind you are good views back to Abridge. Follow the faint path through trees to the otherside and footbridge. Continue with a hedge on your right and later a hedged path as you keep straight ahead to Coopersale Lane, reached beside path sign - Hydes Lane - and the hamlet of Theydon Garnon.

Turn right along the road to the next righthand bend. Here keep ahead following the Monks Walk to All saints church, Theydon Garnon. Walk through the churchyard, passing the church on your left to the drive, church hall and parking area. Turn right to rejoin Coopersale Lane. Turn left and descend to the Hobbs Cross Road. Cross to your left to a bridlepath sign. Follow the track past the Industrial Estate and Hobbs Cross Farm, and join the tarmaced farm drive. Follow it left to pass under the M25. Continue straight ahead, now on a track, and the line of a former Roman Road. Keep the hedge on the right as you walk past Barbers Wood on the left. Gently ascend to a drive and road with North Farm on the immediate left and now in Theydon Mount. Turn right and continue ascending along the road passing a lodge on the right. Then on the left is Taruns Farm and Brickfield Cottages. Now level walking as you pass the private drive to Hill Hall and later Garden Cottage on the right. Continue, and 1/4 mile later reach St. Michael's church on the right, with a good view of Hill Hall. Continue along the road and pass Stoller Lake on the right and cross the M25 road bridge.

Immediately afterwards and as path signed, turn right into the Abridge Golf & Country Club course. First keep left past Hole no. 12 and bear right as marked. Pass Hole 16 and follow a grassy path and cross a fairway to reach the road with Skinners Farm to the right. Opposite is the entrance to Norton Trout Fishery. Cross the road to the next path sign and follow the defined path half right to a footbridge and then around the field edge with electric poles on the right to a stile and footbridge. Follow the field edge right and later left to reach the prominent footbridge over the River Roding - *see photo on page 73*. As you near it, ahead to your left is Stapleford Aerodrome. Cross the bridge and gain the A113, Ongar Road.

Turn right and soon left, as path signed, to pass Patch Park Garden Centre (Cafe) and continue ahead on the drive, passing the Mayhem paint ball complex on the left. Just after turn right - Abridge Country Walk. Follow the wide path to a squeeze stile and onto Church Lane. Turn left and pass Lambourne House. Follow the lane to the church dedicated to All Saints, 1/2 mile away, following it right past Lambourne Hall Cottage. Opposite the church and is Lambourne Hall. Keep ahead a little further and turn right as path signed - Scapley's Wood. Follow the path to a stile and then beside Scapley's Wood on the left to a kissing gate. Bear slightly left to continue on the path to a footbridge and stile. Keep ahead to another kissing gate and New Farm Drive on the edge of Abridge. Turn right passing the farm House and Alderswood Barns. Pass the houses of Abridge to reach the main A113 road. Turn left and pass the Prince of Wales Cottages and back to Roding Hall and on past the Blue Boar Inn to Hoe Lane on the left. A few metres along the main road is the Log Cabin Cafe and Maltsers Arms.

All Saints church, Theydon Garnon.

77

Inside All Saints church, Theydon Garnon, showing the octagonal wooden pillars.

THEYDON GARNON - All Saints church dates from the 13th. century and has a magnificent timber roof, known for its notched lap joints, and dates from this time. Part of the church has octagonal oak columns, instead of stone pillars and were made from wood from Epping Forest. The North aisle dates from 1664 and the date can be seen prominently of the brickwork, outside. Near the chancel can be seen a brass to William Kyrkeby who was Rector of Theydon Garnon between 1442 - 1458 - *photo opposite*. The Tudor tower was built in 1520. The church is one of the most interesting in the area and well worth exploring fully. There was a Priory here and you walked along the *"Monks Walk"* to get here.

HILL HALL - The Elizabethan building is owned by the Crown and in the care of English Heritage. Access is very restricted, as there are today, many private apartments. The original hall was built - 1569-75, by the Smyth (Smith) family during Queen Elizabeth Ist reign, when he was Ambassador to France. The Smith family lived here until the 1850's. The grounds were designed by Repton in 1791. During WW2 it was used as a prisoner of war camp and afterwards a woman's prison until a fire in 1969 badly damaged the building. Inside are some late 16th. century wall-paintings said to be, *"The most important survival of Elizabethan decorative figure painting in England."* The Grade I listed hall and area are part of a Conservation Area.

ST, MICHAEL CHURCH - The earlier church was destroyed by lightning in 1611. The present church was built by Sir William Smith of Hill Hall in 1614. Inside is a monument to Sir Thomas Smith, Sir William's uncle, who died in 1577, when the hall was being rebuilt.

Lambourne House.

Norman doorway.

ST. MARY & ALL SAINTS CHURCH, LAMBOURNE END

- On the outside can be seen the remains of a Norman doorway. The interior is full of monuments to owners of the halls in the area, which make up the scattered village of Lambourne, which accounts for the church's isolated position. Originally the parish covered 2,471 acres. Part of the church is 13th. century and the bell tower, 16th. century. Much was rebuilt in the 18th. century. Inside is part of a medieval painting of St. Christopher, the Patron Saint of Travellers. There are several monuments to the Lookwood family, with the words - Resurgam - *"I shall rise again."*

St. Mary & All Saints, Lambourne End.

Lambourne Hall.

WALTHAM ABBEY, WARLIES PARK & UPSHIRE - 6 MILES

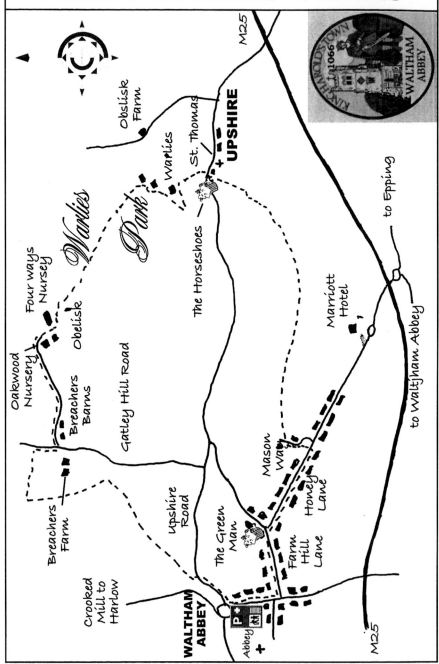

WALTHAM ABBEY

KING HAROLD'S TOWN 1066

M25

UPSHIRE

St. Thomas

Warlies

Obelisk Farm

to Epping

Warlies

Park

Four ways Nursey

Marriott Hotel

The Horseshoes

Oakwood Nursery

Obelisk

Breachers Barns

Gatley Hill Road

to Waltham Abbey

Breachers Farm

Mason Way

Honey Lane

Upshire Road

The Green Man

Farm Hill Lane

Crooked Mill to Harlow

WALTHAM ABBEY

Abbey P

M25

82

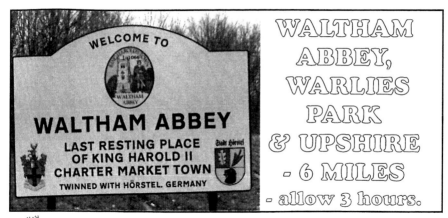

WALTHAM ABBEY, WARLIES PARK & UPSHIRE - 6 MILES - allow 3 hours.

Basic route - Waltham Abbey Gardens Car Park - Upshire Road - Breachers Farm - Breachers Barns - Four Ways Nursery - Warlies Park - Warlies - Upshire - Trout Farm - Honey Lane - Waltham Abbey.

Map - O.S. 1:25,000 Explorer Series No. 174 - Epping Forest & Lee Valley.

Car Park & Start - Waltham Abbey Gardens Car Park, just off the roadabout - Crooked Mile/Waltham Abbey/Upshire roads. Grid Ref. 382008.

Inns - The Horseshoes, Upshire. The Green Man, Farm Hill Road, Waltham Abbey. The New Inn, Waltham Abbey.

Cafe - Teas in Waltham Abbey, close to the church/abbey remains; 3 mins from the car park.

ABOUT THE WALK - The principal aim of the walk is to explore Warlies Park, owned by the Corporation of London. It is a sanctuary close to Waltham Abbey and Upshire with an exceptional house. Deer are frequently seen. The route uses reasonably signed paths but some paths are infrequently used. You have fine views of the London skyline as you cross some the highest land in Essex. Passing nurseries you reach Warlies Park and cross it to the impressive Warlies Park House, and ascend to Upshire with an inn. In St. Thomas churchyard the Realty TV star Jane Goody is buried. You descend and follow a grassy swathe between the houses of Waltham Abbey back to the town and pass the Green Man Inn. A pleasant walk in a lesser known walking area, full of interest. Waltham Abbey is well worth a visit, after the walk!

WALKING INSTRUCTIONS - Follow the car park path, left, to the main road and cross. Turn left and pass St. Clements and right along the Upshire Road. Walk along the righthand side for 4 minutes to where the road curves right. Look out on the left for a yellow topped footpath marker post above the embankment. Cross the road to it and onto a footbridge. The path is defined across a field and onto another footbridge and marker post. The path continues straight ahead, but it maybe more practical to follow the field edge at this point. Follow the edge left and right and ascend to trees. Turn left, as path arrowed and basically keep along the crest with trees on the right. To your left are views southward to London's skyline. Pass another marker post and turn left and right to continue by a fence with Breachers Farm to the right. Continue to a wide fenced track on the right. Turn right down this to Galleyhill Road.

Turn right and ascend. 3 mins later, turn left along a single tracked road - Breachers Barn Lane. Pass The Barns and Dallance House Farm and continue to Oakwood Nursery, nearly 1/2 mile from the road. As path signed turn right to Four Ways Nursery. Reaching the buildings and bungalow turn left and then right to gain a path along the perimeter edge. Follow this to a stile and onto a gate. Turn right and keep beside the hedge on your left with a brick obelisk on the right. In the lefthand corner of the field reach a gate and turn left and shortly afterwards right to a footbridge and gate beyond beside an information board about Warlies Park.

Turn half left and follow the defined path to two stile gates. Continue diagonally across the field to the far lefthand corner and another gate. Through keep to the righthand path to reach the drive and bridlepath sign close to Warlies Gardens house. Turn right along the track/drive and pass houses on the left. Reaching the first entrance to Warlies keep right along the drive to the next entrance with a stile and path sign. Turn left and as you near the impressive house, turn right to a stile. Ascend the field towards Upshire and as you do so look back at the columned south front of Warlies. Beyond can be seen the Temple. Reach a stile and car park of The Horseshoes Inn. Gaining the road - Horseshoe Hill - to the left is St. Thomas church. Turn right and left to the fenced path immediately before The Horseshoes Inn, path signed - Woodgreen Road.

Follow the path down soon with a hedge on your left to a footbridge. Turn right to another and then left with the hedge on your right and reach Woodgreen Road. Cross, as footpath signed and follow the path left and right - hedged path to a stile. Continue with the hedge on the right to another stile.

Here you should keep ahead but with electric fences it is impractical and no stiles. I turned half left to the field entrance with Dillons Fishing Lake on the left. Turn right along the path to where it turns left. Here, below, on the right is a field entrance and aim for the immediate left of a communication mast. Here you pick up the defined path again. Pass through the hedge and turn left with the hedge on the left. Soon after turn turn left and right and continue with the hedge on the right. You are now approaching the houses of Waltham Abbey. Turn left and right again to pass the end of houses on the left and others to your right. You have now reached a grassy swathe which you follow all the way for nearly 1/2 mile. Immediately pass Longfields Allotments Site on the left. Soon after turn left and right and cross a footbridge and continue ahead along the grass. Keep straight ahead and cross a concrete path and continue to shops on the right. Continue ahead past a football field on the right to Mason Way.

Turn left and where the road turns left, keep ahead on a tarmaced path and ascend to reach Honey Lane. Turn right and follow the road to the junction with Farm Hill Road, opposite the Green Man Inn. Turn left to reach the main road opposite the New Inn in Waltham Abbey. Cross and turn right and soon on the left is the path back into Abbey Gardens Car park.

Brick obelisk near Four Ways Nursery.

WARLIES PARK - Bought by the Corporation of London in 1986. The parkland is home to fallow deer, part of our pastoral heritage. The park has several old oak trees and an 18th. century Rotunda, named as the Temple on the O.S. Map.

The Bachelor Wing, Warlies Park House.

WARLIES PARK HOUSE - 18th. century Grade 11 listed building and part of the Upshire Conservation Area. In the 14th. century the area was owned by Richard de Warley. By the 18th. century it was owned by the Morgan family who eventually owned 477 acres. Later owned by the Buxton's and in 1915 became part of Dr. Barnado's homes and used as a school. The Bachelor Wing dates from about 1880 and the columned Georgian Wing about 1860.

The Georgian Wing.

ST. THOMAS CHURCH, UPSHIRE - The churchyard extension is a lasting memorial to, *"Our brother, Leslie John Padfield, who died whilst a prisoner of war in 1942, and his comrades who gave their lives in 1939/45 war."*
Jade Goody, the realty TV star, is buried here, near the top.

WALTHAM ABBEY - Although off the route it is well worth exploring. The Abbey ruins, the Norman Abbey church and resting place of King Harold, who died from an arrow in his eye, in 1066.

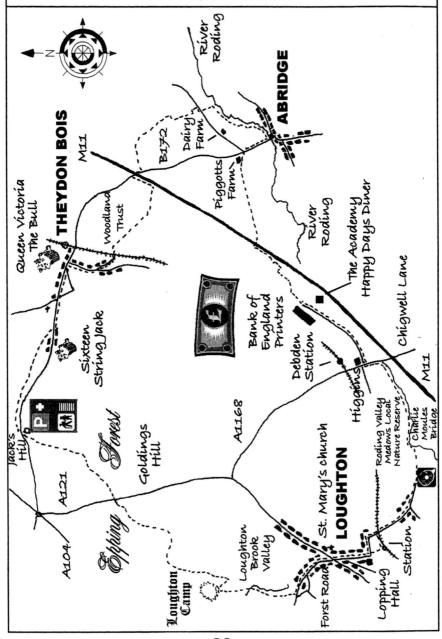

EPPING FOREST, LOUGHTON, ABRIDGE & THEYDON BOIS
- 12 MILES
- allow 5 hours.

Basic route - Jack's Hill Car park - Epping Forest - Goldings Hill - Loughton Camp - Loughton Brook Valley - Loughton - Roding Valley Meadows Local Nature Reserve - M11 - Piggotts Farm - Abridge - M11 - Woodland Trust - Theydon Bois - Epping Forest - Jack's Hill Car Park.

Map - O.S. 1:25,000 Explorer Series No. 174 - Epping Forest & Lee Valley.

Car park and start - Jack's Hill Epping Forest Car Park; south side. Beside the B172 Theydon Bois Road. Grid Ref. 435996. Alternative starts - Broadstrood Car park, on Goldings Hill, beside the A121; in Loughton, Abridge and Theydon Bois.

Inns - Royal Oak, Victoria Tavern, Carpenter Arms & The Hollybush; Loughton. The Blue Boar, The Maltsers Arms; Abridge, 200 m. from the route. The Bull, Queen Victoria, Sixteen String Jack (just off the route); Theydon Bois.

Cafe - Loughton. The Log Cabin, Abridge, 1/4 mile from the route.

ABOUT THE WALK - The longest walk in the book but one that explores the southern end of the area. A complete mixed bag of walking and countryside with many surprises. The first four miles are through Epping Forest with a side trip to the Iron Age, Loughton Camp. You pass through Loughton and numerous inns, before walking through the Roding Valley Meadows Local Nature Reserve. After passing the Bank of England printing works, you return to countryside and cross the M11 to reach Abridge; inns and cafe just off the route. Following good paths you pass under the M11 and reach the Woodlands Trust Theydon Bois site before reaching the village. The Green is a gem as you walk out of the village back into Epping Forest and the brief ascent back to Jack's Hill. A stunning circuit, rich in diversity.

WALKING INSTRUCTIONS - Starting from Jack's Hill Car Park, pass the Information board and bar gate and follow the wide path/track for basically 8 mins. in Epping Forest, to the first path/track on the right. Turn right along this and soon descend Furze Ground (meaning gorse) and later ascend to the A121 road at Goldings Hill, beside Broadstrood Car park. Cross and continue on the path/track into Great Monk Wood. Soon descend and curve right, ascending and after approximately 14 mins from the A121 road, reach a track on the right (Centenary Way) and one on the left (Clay Ride) soon after. Continue straight ahead for about 4 mins to where the path descends. Here you can turn right and follow a small path to Loughton Camp. Walk left around it to a history board and turn left to descend a wide path back to the main path, lower down. If you keep straight ahead instead of visiting Loughton Vamp, both routes meet near the end of the descent. Keep on the main path passing Loughton Brook and Valley on the left. Ascend for 80 metres to the first wide path on the left. Turn left and follow this to the forest edge and road - Earl's Path. Turn right and left to walk along Forest Road into Loughton. Pass three inns - Royal Oak, Victoria Tavern and Carpenter Arms. Also, house no. 116 has a blue plaque to the poet Barker who was born here. Continue to the crossroads in Loughton, beside the unusual road sign, with almost equidistant - 4 1/4 miles - from Epping, Abridge and Waltham Abbey.

Cross the road with the Hollybush Inn to the right and St. Mary's church on the left. Walk along Station Road and pass Lopping Hall on the right with a woodland lopping tympanum. Pass Sainsbury's on the right and where the road turns left - Alderton Hill - you can either keep ahead, as path signed to the Underground Station and then left to Roding Road.

Alternatively turn left along Alderton Hill and pass Roding Valley High School with a historic blue plaque. Turn right into Roding Road and pass under the underground line; it is here the station path rejoins the route. Continue along the road and pass St. Michael's church on the right to reach traffic lights. Bear half left to continue along South View Road. Follow it to its end to a recreation ground and tennis courts.

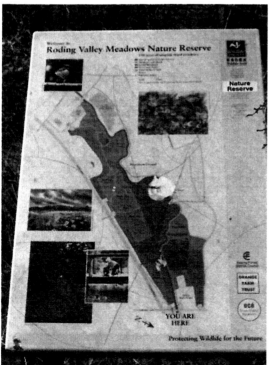

Turn left and right to pass the tennis courts and then diagonally half left across the area, past the football field on the left to the River Roding and the Charlie Moules Bridge. Don't cross, but turn left along the path and now in the Roding Valley Meadows Local Nature Reserve. Follow the path left and soon turn right to continue on the path keeping close to the river on the right. Pass path sign - To Chigwell Lane; your destination. Reach a kissing gate and Nature Reserve board before Chigwell Lane.

Turn left and pass Debden Sports Club on the left and turn right into Langston

Road infront of the prominent building, Higgins, which you have seen from afar. Follow the road past industrial complexes and in 1/2 mile on the right is The Academy and Happy Days Diner. On the left is High Security fence of the De La Rue, Bank of England printing works. Follow the road to where it curves left. Here on the right is the signed fenced path. Reach a footbridge and bear right towards a wood and bear left along its edge towards another. Here turn right and left to pass the other wood and gain a field. Keep to the righthand side and now near the M11 to a track and farm bridge over the motorway. Turn right across it and follow the track to Piggotts farm, 1/2 mile away. Use stiles past the house, on the right, and beside the drive to the B172 road - Abridge Road.

Cross and turn right along the pavement to just before the bridge over the River Roding. If wanting to visit Abridge, cross the bridge and turn right to reach the two inns and the Log Cabin Cafe a little further along the main road. Before the bridge, as path signed, turn left and keep to the field edge. Continue close to the river with Dairy Farm to your left. Towards the end of the second field the stile is in the lefthand corner. Turn left and continue beside the hedge on your right to Epping Road. Turn right and moments later left, as path signed. First with the field edge on your left for a few yards before turning left and right to continue the hedge on your right. Soon turn right across a footbridge and then left to continue with hedge and stream on your left to another footbridge. Continue by the hedge and follow it left to Abridge Road beneath the M11.

Turn right and pass under the motorway and immediately left, as path signed. The path, at first keeps close to the fence on the left, near the M11, as you are now in the Theydon Bois Woodland Trust site. Reach a path post and turn right past a solitary oak tree and across an open field, bear left to the woodland track and another Woodland Trust Board and seat. Before it turn right to a kissing gate and continue with the hedge on your left to a footbridge. Here you turn right and left to continue and ascend slightly using stiles to reach the bridge over the Underground line. Cross and keep to the lefthand road as you enter the edge of Theydon Bois, walking along Green Glade. Reach Theydon Park Road and turn right to pass the edge of the Green and pond to the shopping area and B172 road. Across to the right is The Bull Inn.

Turn left along the road passing the Queen Victoria with the Green on the left. In 1/4 mile pass St. Mary's church and the Old School dated 1840. Continue along the road a little further to an open grassy space on the right; part of Epping Forest. Here gain a path along its edge near the road. Soon its turns right, but just ahead up the road is the Sixteen String Jack Inn. Follow the ascending wide path past houses on the left at first and in almost 1/2 mile reach a small car park on the left. Continue on the path near the road for 1/4 mile to the next car park and Green Ride. Turn left to the B172 road and cross back into Jack's Hill Car Park where you began.

LOUGHTON CAMP - The earth banks surround an enclosure of more than four hectares. The banks originally would have been 3 metres high with a 3 metre deep ditch. Made mostly by hand in about 500 BC. Primarily used to secure the cattle during times of conflict.

GEORGE GRANVILLE BARKER 1913-1991 - Poet, was born here. He wrote and had published many poems and for awhile was professor of English Literature in 1939 in Japan. Later moved to America and then back to England to live in Norfolk. In 1950 his novel, *"The Dead Seagull"*, was published. Robert Frasher write his biography - *"The Chameleon Poet: A Life of George Barker."*

LOPPING HALL - Built in 1884. The hall was built out of the compensation for Lopping Rights in Epping Forest, when the City of London won a legal battle to preserve Epping Forest. Today the forest - here only 12 miles from central London, is a remarkable jewel of woodland surrounded by the sprawl of London.

THEYDON BOIS WOODLAND TRUST SITE - A new forest covering 93 acres. In 2008 I joined Buddhist monks from London and helped plant 1,400 trees here!

Tree planting in the Woodland Trust site, Theydon Bois.

THEYDON BOIS - Pronounced *"Thaydon Boys"*. Magnificent green, which has been a local tourist attraction for Londoners, being 20 miles from central London. In the early 1900's, visitor's could buy a stone with the name Theydon Bois on, as a souvenir.

The Bull Inn, Theydon Bois.

SIXTEEN STRING JACK - Real name John Rann - 1750-1774. A colourful highwayman born near Bath, Somerset. Began life as a pick pocket but graduated to highway robbery; for which Epping Forest was notorious. Although arrested six times and brought to trail, the cases failed upon lack of evidence. Finally he was caught robbing the chaplain of Princess Amelia near Brentford in 1774. He was known for his colourful clothes and life style, and wore eight coloured strings on each knee of his silk breeches. At his execution at Tyburn on November 30th 1774, he wore a pea green suit, danced a jig and chatted to the crowd and hangman before being hung. A novel on his life was published in 1841 - *"Sixteen String Jack"*.

WALK
RECORD PAGE

Matching Green & High Laver - 9 1/2 miles ....

Epping Green and Latton Priory - 7 miles ....

Epping Green and Nazeing - 5 1/2 miles ....

Around North Weald Bassett - 6 miles ....

Chipping Ongar, Greensted Green, Bobbingworth & Moreton - 10 miles ....

Chipping Ongar and Fyfield - 8 miles ....

Chipping Ongar, Greensted, Clatterford End and Stanford Rivers - 6 miles ....

Toot Hill, Log Church & Chipping Ongar - 6 miles ....

Coopersale (Epping) & Ongar Park - 10 miles ....

Abridge, Theydon Garnon & Hill Hall - 9 1/2 miles ....

Waltham Abbey, Warlies Park & Upshire - 6 miles ....

Epping Forest, Loughton, Abridge & Theydon Bois - 12 miles ....

THE JOHN MERRILL WALK BADGE

Complete SIX walks in this book and get the above special embroidered badge and signed certificate. Badges are Black cloth with lettering and hiker embroidered in four colours.

BADGE ORDER FORM

Date walks completed..

NAME ....

ADDRESS ....

....

Price: £6.00 each including postage, packing, VAT and signed completion certificate. Amount enclosed (Payable to The John Merrill Foundation).

From: The John Merrill Foundation,
32, Holmesdale, Waltham Cross,
Hertsfordshire, EN8 8QY

Fax/Tel - 01992 - 762776
E-mail - john@thejohnmerrillministry.co.uk

HAPPY WALKING T SHIRT - £10 inc. P&P

********** YOU MAY PHOTOCOPY THIS FORM **********

As I walk ....

I am not aware of my feet touching the earth, but am always looking ahead surveying the ground and intuitively place my feet where necessary. I look at all my surroundings, the hedges, trees, flowers and stop and observe the birds and animals that cross my path.

I see the wren calling in the hedgerows. I see the wild flowers growing throughout the seasons. I hear the call of a green woodpecker that sweeps ahead of me across the field. I near a scratching squirrel and call to it and watch him watching me briefly, before running and leaping effortless to a tree and up its bark. I follow and watch him hiding and ascending the tree, before swinging off onto another tree branch. I surprise a pheasant, who surprises us both and shrieks taking to the air urgently. I stop and admire a bee orchid growing alone on the field edge, knowing it is rare and must not be picked, for it will die.

I follow the path down to a brook and cross the footbridge and stop and gaze at the water to see if anything moves here or along the banks. Sometimes I see a fish, a water vole and occasionally a kingfisher - a mere flash of blue, but nevertheless a wondrous sight. I walk further and as I round a bend in the path in woodland, I surprise six roe deer who prick their ears, snort, and run away only to stop moments later to look again at this intruder in their world.

I marvel at these sights and sounds, which make me both joyful and humble at seeing the living unspoilt world, of which we all connected.

I walk beside a barbed wire fence and notice the sheep's wool caught on the barbs, as they either squeezed through or reached for a succulent piece of grass.

I watch the trees sway in the light breeze, the leaves flutter gently. I gaze at the fluffy clouds that glide across the sky. I walk in the cool damp air, but all is enjoyable and serene. Then suddenly the sun appears, and for a brief moment, illuminates my world and can see everything in its vibrant colours. As though showing me what is there and be patient. The clouds roll in and I am left with the magic of those priceless seconds. My heart is full of love for sharing this moment.

I walk on just looking and admiring all that my eyes see. I know I am guided and watched over, for I never put a foot wrong. I just walk with no preconceived ideas and no expectations. I just let it all happened in its own good time, which makes me very blessed at what has occurred.

I visit a church and are humbled at the workmanship and the story of the woodwork, stone and memorials. I touch the font and feel its story and energy.

As I walk though woodland and stop and rest by an oak tree and feel its trunk against my back. I feel its energy and wisdom, and say a prayer and touch it gently with my hand.

As I near the end of the walk I turn and raise my hand and say good-bye and thanks for allowing me to visit and enjoy your surroundings. It has meant much and I shall return to explore further and watch the unfolding kaleidoscope of life that exists there.

I walk and give thanks that I am able to do so with my body and mind. It is all a deep and profound experience without end.

© John Merrill - 9/2/2010

OTHER NORTH LONDON WALK BOOKS
by JOHN N. MERRILL

SHORT CIRCULAR WALKS ON THE RIVER LEE NAVIGATION - Northern Volume -
Ponder's End - Hertford. 64 pages, 23 photographs, 10 detailed maps and walks. History notes.
- ISBN 1-903627-68-0 @ £7.95
WALKING THE RIVER LEE NAVIGATION - VOL 1 & 2.

SHORT CIRCULAR WALKS ON THE NEW RIVER & SOUTH EAST HERTFORDSHIRE
11 walks - 5 to 10 miles long between Waltham Cross and Hertford; many on the New River. New revised and enlarged edition 68 pages, 24 photographs , 13 detailed maps. History notes.
ISBN 1-903627-69-9 @ £7.95

SHORT CIRCULAR WALKS IN EPPING FOREST
10 circular walks 6 to 18 miles long. Combined they explore the whole forest and its surrounding area. 68 pages. 12 maps. 30 photographs. History notes.
ISBN 1-903627-72-9 @ £7.95

LONG CIRCULAR WALKS IN EASTERN HERTFORDSHIRE
9 walks - 15 to 20 miles long. Beautiful unspoilt walking in rolling countryside full of historical interest. £9.95
ISBN 978-0-9553691-7-9

LONG CIRCULAR WALKS IN WESTERN HERTFORDSHIRE
- 9 long walks - 15 to 20 miles..
112 pages. Wire bound. 55 photographs. 20detailed maps.
£9.95 ISBN 978-0-955651113

SHORT CIRCULAR WALKS AROUND HERTFORD.
3 historical Town walks and four country walks.
ISBN 978-0-9556511-7-5 £9.95

SHORT CIRCULAR WALKS ON THE RIVER STORT NAVIGATION
8 circular walks; 1 End to End walk. Full history and photographic study of this peaceful waterway. 92 pages. 68 photographgs. 12 maps. ISBN 1-903627- 73-7 £9.95

SHORT CIRCULAR WALKS ON THE RIVER LEE NAVIGATION - Southern Volume -
Limehouse basin to Hackney Marsh. 5 walks on the Regent Canal, Hertford Union and Limehouse Cut. Including Three Mills and its rivers. The guide also details a 28 mile End to End walk along the Navigation. 68 pages. 10 maps, 30 photographs.
ISBn 1-903627-74-5 £7.95

EPPING FOREST CHALLENGE WALK - 21 MILES.
Starts and ends at Waltham Abbey and takes in the whole forest. 44 pages. 6 maps. 10 photos £6.95
ISBN 978-0-9553691-0-0

"St. ALBANS WAY" - 26 mile Pilgrims walk from Waltham Abbey to St. Alban's Cathedral.
£6.95
ISBN 978-0-9553691-3-1

NORTH LONDON - THE THREE BOROUGH CHALLENGE WALK - 21 MILES
A walk linking together the three boroughs of Enfield, Barnet and Haringey.
A magnificent countryside walk. Certificate for the successful.
A5. 40 pages. Full colour book.
ISBN 978-0-9556511-9-9
£5.95

NEW - SHORT CIRCULAR WALKS AROUND BISHOP'S STORTFORD

THE PILGRIM'S WAY SERIES by Revd. John N. Merrill

THE WALSINGHAM WAY
- Ely to Walsingham - 72 miles - 1-903627-33-8 ....£8.95
- 56 pages and 40 photographs.

THE WALSINGHAM WAY
- King's Lynn to Walsingham - 35 miles - 1-903627-41 - 9 ....£9.95
- 72 pages and 50 colour photographs.

TURN LEFT AT GRANJA DE LA MORERUELA
- 700 miles - Seville to Santiago de Compostela, Spain. 1-903627 - 40 - 0 ....£14.95..
- 172 pages and 120 photographs

NORTH TO SANTIAGO DE COMPOSTELA VIA FATIMA -
1-903627- 44 - 3 - 650 miles from Lagos, Algarve, through Portugal via Fatima to Santiago de
Compostela........£17.95.. - 220 pages and 160 photographs

ST. OLAV'S WAY - 400 MILES - NORWAY
- Photgraphic book and basic guide ...1 - 903627- 45 - 1..........£12.95
- 124 pages and 130 photographs.

ST. WINEFRIDE'S WAY - 14 miles - St. Asaph to Holywell.
ISBN 1-903627-66-4   40 pages. 5 maps. 20 photographs..£6.95

ST. ALBAN'S WAY - 25 mile walk from Waltham Abbey to St. Alban's Cathedral.
Linking together two major medieval pilgrimage centres.
ISBN 978-0-9553691-3-1 48 Pages. 7 maps. 18 colour photographs. £7.95

ST. KENELM'S TRAIL by John Price - From the Clent Hills to Winchcombe Abbey - 60
miles. ISBN 978-0-9553691-6-2 . 60 pages 5 maps....£7.50

DERBYSHIRE PILGRIMAGES - The pilgrimage routes, saints and hermits of the county
and Peak District. Plus a St. Bertram Walk and about a pilgrimage.
48 pages. £5.95

LONDON TO ST. ALBANS - 36 MILES ......NEW....... ISBN 978-0-9560649-7-4
80 pages. Wire bound. 45 photos. 8 maps. A stunning walk from Westminster to St. Albans via
32 churches. £9.95

FOLKESTONE, HYTHE TO CANTERBURY - 25 MILES ..NEW
ISBN 9780956606498 1.............68 pages. 40 colour phots. 8 maps. £9.95

LONDON TO CANTERBURY - 75 MILES.
ISBN 9780956064967 140 pages. 146 PHOTOS. 15 maps..................£12.95

LONDON TO WALSINGHAM - 190 MILES
ISBN 9780956464422..................256pages. 250 photos. 40 maps. ...£14.95

THE JOHN SCHORNE PEREGRINATION by Michael Mooney. 27 mile walk in
Buckinghamshire to North Marston, the site of medieval miracles and pilgrimage.
A5. 56 pages. 16 colour photographs. 8 maps. £7.95
ISBN 978-0-9564644-0-8

ST CEDD'S PILGRIMAGE - 24 MILES -To St. Peter's Chapel on the Wall, near Bradwell on
Sea. ISBN 978-0-9564644-7-7. 56 pages. A5 24 colour photos. 4 maps. £6.94

ST BIRINIUS PILGRIMAGE - 26 MILES - To his shrine in Dorchester Abbey, Oxfordshire.
ISBN 978-0-9564644-8-4 56 pages. 20 colour photos. 8 maps. £6.95

PILGRIM'S PASSPORT - ISBN 978-0-9568044-1-9 Specially designed book to record your
sello s. £5.00

OUR LADY OF ULTING PILGRIMAGE WALK - 16 MILES - To a former Marian shrine is
Essex, near Maldon. ISBN 978-0-9568044-5-7   £6.95

OUR LADY OF CAVERSHAM PILGRIMAGE WALK - 38 MILES - Windsor to Reading.
A5 wire bound. 80 pages. Maps and photos. £8.95   ISBN 978-0-9568044-6-4

MANDEVILLE MONKS WAY - 42 MILES - Edmonton Green (N. London) to Saffron Walden.
A5 Wire bound. 80 pages. Maps and photo's. £8.95. ISBN 978-0-9568044-7-1

THE ESSEX PRIORY WAY - 20 MILES - St. Osyth to Colchester, linking St/ Osyth Priory
and St. Botoloph's Priory together. Beautiful coastal walk. ISBN 978-0-9568044-8-8 £8.50

WALKING THE CAMINO DI ASSISI - 320 KM - My story of walking this route, following
in the footsteps of St. Francis and his life story. A5. Wire bound 94 pages. 80 photos.   £9.95
ISBN 978-0-9574186-2-2

AYLESFORD PILGRIMAGE - 13 miles from Rochester Cathedral to The Friars, Aylesford.
see my website - **www.thejohnmerrillministry.co.uk**

OTHER BOOKS by Revd. John N. Merrill

CIRCULAR WALK GUIDES -

SHORT CIRCULAR WALKS IN THE PEAK DISTRICT - Vols. 1 to 9
CIRCULAR WALKS IN WESTERN PEAKLAND
SHORT CIRCULAR WALKS IN THE STAFFORDSHIRE MOORLANDS
SHORT CIRCULAR WALKS - TOWNS & VILLAGES OF THE PEAK DISTRICT
SHORT CIRCULAR WALKS AROUND MATLOCK
SHORT CIRCULAR WALKS IN "PEAK PRACTICE COUNTRY."
SHORT CIRCULAR WALKS IN THE DUKERIES
SHORT CIRCULAR WALKS IN SOUTH YORKSHIRE
SHORT CIRCULAR WALKS IN SOUTH DERBYSHIRE
SHORT CIRCULAR WALKS AROUND BUXTON
SHORT CIRCULAR WALKS AROUND WIRKSWORTH
SHORT CIRCULAR WALKS IN THE HOPE VALLEY
40 SHORT CIRCULAR WALKS IN THE PEAK DISTRICT
CIRCULAR WALKS ON KINDER & BLEAKLOW
SHORT CIRCULAR WALKS IN SOUTH NOTTINGHAMSHIRE
SHORT CIRCULAR WALKS IN CHESHIRE
SHORT CIRCULAR WALKS IN WEST YORKSHIRE
WHITE PEAK DISTRICT AIRCRAFT WRECKS
CIRCULAR WALKS IN THE DERBYSHIRE DALES
SHORT CIRCULAR WALKS FROM BAKEWELL
SHORT CIRCULAR WALKS IN LATHKILL DALE
CIRCULAR WALKS IN THE WHITE PEAK
SHORT CIRCULAR WALKS IN EAST DEVON
SHORT CIRCULAR WALKS AROUND HARROGATE
SHORT CIRCULAR WALKS IN CHARNWOOD FOREST
SHORT CIRCULAR WALKS AROUND CHESTERFIELD
SHORT CIRCULAR WALKS IN THE YORKS DALES - Vol 1 - Southern area.
SHORT CIRCULAR WALKS IN THE AMBER VALLEY (Derbyshire)
SHORT CIRCULAR WALKS IN THE LAKE DISTRICT
SHORT CIRCULAR WALKS IN THE NORTH YORKSHIRE MOORS
SHORT CIRCULAR WALKS IN EAST STAFFORDSHIRE
LONG CIRCULAR WALKS IN THE PEAK DISTRICT - Vol.1 to 5.
DARK PEAK AIRCRAFT WRECK WALKS
LONG CIRCULAR WALKS IN THE STAFFORDSHIRE MOORLANDS
LONG CIRCULAR WALKS IN CHESHIRE
WALKING THE TISSINGTON TRAIL
WALKING THE HIGH PEAK TRAIL
WALKING THE MONSAL TRAIL & SETT VALLEY TRAILS
PEAK DISTRICT WALKING - TEN "TEN MILER'S" - Vol 1 and 2.
CLIMB THE PEAKS OF THE PEAK DISTRICT
PEAK DISTRICT WALK A MONTH Vols One,Two, Three, Four, Five & Six
TRAIN TO WALK Vol. One - The Hope Valley Line
DERBYSHIRE LOST VILLAGE WALKS -Vol One and Two.
CIRCULAR WALKS IN DOVEDALE AND THE MANIFOLD VALLEY
CIRCULAR WALKS AROUND GLOSSOP
WALKING THE LONGDENDALE TRAIL
WALKING THE UPPER DON TRAIL
SHORT CIRCULAR WALKS IN CANNOCK CHASE
CIRCULAR WALKS IN THE DERWENT VALLEY
WALKING THE TRAILS OF NORTH-EAST DERBYSHIRE
WALKING THE PENNINE BRIDLEWAY & CIRCULAR WALKS
SHORT CIRCULAR WALKS ON THE NEW RIVER & SOUTH-EAST HERTFORDSHIRE
SHORT CIRCULAR WALKS IN EPPING FOREST

WALKING THE STREETS OF LONDON
LONG CIRCULAR WALKS IN EASTERN HERTFORDSHIRE
LONG CIRCULAR WALKS IN WESTERN HERTFORDSHIRE
WALKS IN THE LONDON BOROUGH OF ENFIELD
WALKS IN THE LONDON BOROUGH OF BARNET
WALKS IN THE LONDON BOROUGH OF HARINGEY
WALK IN THE LONDON BOROUGH OF WALTHAM FOREST
SHORT CIRCULAR WALKS AROUND HERTFORD
THE BIG WALKS OF LONDON
SHORT CIRCULAR WALKS AROUND BISHOP'S STORTFORD
SHORT CIRCULAR WALKS AROUND EPPING DISTRICT
CIRCULAR WALKS IN THE BOROUGH OF BROXBOURNE
LONDON INTERFAITH WALKS - Vol 1 and Vol. 2
LONG CIRCULAR WALKS IN THE NORTH CHILTERNS
SHORT CIRCULAR WALKS IN EASTERN HERTFORDSHIRE
WORCESTERSHIRE VILLAGE WALKS by Des Wright
WARWICKSHIRE VILLAGE WALKS by Des Wright
WALKING AROUND THE ROYAL PARKS OF LONDON
WALKS IN THE LONDON BOROUGH OF CHELSEA AND ROYAL KENSINGTON

CANAL WALKS -

VOL 1 - DERBYSHIRE & NOTTINGHAMSHIRE
VOL 2 - CHESHIRE & STAFFORDSHIRE
VOL 3 - STAFFORDSHIRE
VOL 4 - THE CHESHIRE RING
VOL 5 - THE GRANTHAM CANAL
VOL 6 - SOUTH YORKSHIRE
VOL 7 - THE TRENT & MERSEY CANAL
VOL 8 - WALKING THE DERBY CANAL RING
VOL 9 - WALKING THE LLANGOLLEN CANAL
VOL 10 - CIRCULAR WALKS ON THE CHESTERFIELD CANAL
VOL 11 - CIRCULAR WALKS ON THE CROMFORD CANAL
Vol.13 - SHORT CIRCULAR WALKS ON THE RIVER LEE NAVIGATION -Vol. 1 - North
Vol. 14 - SHORT CIRCULAR WALKS ON THE RIVER STORT NAVIGATION
Vol.15 - SHORT CIRCULAR WALKS ON THE RIVER LEE NAVIGATION - Vol. 2 - South
Vol. 16 - WALKING THE CANALS OF LONDON
Vol 17 - WALKING THE RIVER LEE NAVIGATION
Vol. 20 - SHORT CIRCULAR WALKS IN THE COLNE VALLEY
Vol 21 - THE BLACKWATER & CHELMER NAVIGATION - End to End.
Vol. 22 - NOTTINGHAM'S LOST CANAL by Bernard Chell.
Vol. 23 - WALKING THE RIVER WEY & GODALMING NAVIAGTIONS END TO END
Vol.25 - WALKING THE GRAND UNION CANAL - LONDON TO BIRMINGHAM.

JOHN MERRILL DAY CHALLENGE WALKS

WHITE PEAK CHALLENGE WALK
THE HAPPY HIKER - WHITE PEAK - CHALLENGE WALK
DARK PEAK CHALLENGE WALK
PEAK DISTRICT END TO END WALKS
STAFFORDSHIRE MOORLANDS CHALLENGE WALK

JOHN MERRILL DAY CHALLENGE WALKS

WHITE PEAK CHALLENGE WALK
THE HAPPY HIKER - WHITE PEAK - CHALLENGE WALK No.2
DARK PEAK CHALLENGE WALK
PEAK DISTRICT END TO END WALKS
STAFFORDSHIRE MOORLANDS CHALLENGE WALK
THE LITTLE JOHN CHALLENGE WALK
YORKSHIRE DALES CHALLENGE WALK
NORTH YORKSHIRE MOORS CHALLENGE WALK
LAKELAND CHALLENGE WALK
THE RUTLAND WATER CHALLENGE WALK
MALVERN HILLS CHALLENGE WALK
THE SALTERIS WAY
THE SNOWDON CHALLENGE
CHARNWOOD FOREST CHALLENGE WALK
THREE COUNTIES CHALLENGE WALK (Peak District).
CAL-DER-WENT WALK
THE QUANTOCK WAY
BELVOIR WITCHES CHALLENGE WALK
THE CARNEDDAU CHALLENGE WALK
THE SWEET PEA CHALLENGE WALK
THE LINCOLNSHIRE WOLDS - BLACK DEATH - CHALLENGE WALK
JENNIFER'S CHALLENGE WALK
THE EPPING FOREST CHALLENGE WALK
THE THREE BOROUGH CHALLENGE WALK - NORTH LONDON
THE HERTFORD CHALLENGE WALK
THE BOSHAM CHALLENGE WALK
THE KING JOHN CHALLENGE WALK
THE NORFOLK BROADS CHALLENGE WALK
THE RIVER MIMRAM WALK
THE ISLE OF THANET CHHALENGE WALK

INSTRUCTION & RECORD -

HIKE TO BE FIT.....STROLLING WITH JOHN
THE JOHN MERRILL WALK RECORD BOOK
HIKE THE WORLD - John Merrill's guide to walking & Backpacking.

MULTIPLE DAY WALKS -

THE RIVERS'S WAY
PEAK DISTRICT: HIGH LEVEL ROUTE
PEAK DISTRICT MARATHONS
THE LIMEY WAY
THE PEAKLAND WAY
COMPO'S WAY by Alan Hiley
THE BRIGHTON WAY

COAST WALKS & NATIONAL TRAILS -

ISLE OF WIGHT COAST PATH
PEMBROKESHIRE COAST PATH
THE CLEVELAND WAY
WALKING ANGELSEY'S COASTLINE.
WALKING THE COASTLINE OF THE CHANNEL ISLANDS
THE ISLE OF MAN COASTAL PATH - "The Way of the Gull."
A WALK AROUND HAYLING ISLAND
A WALK AROUND THE ISLE OF SHEPPEY
A WALK AROUND THE ISLE OF JERSEY
WALKING AROUND THE ISLANDS OF ESSEX

DERBYSHIRE & PEAK DISTRICT HISTORICAL GUIDES -

A to Z GUIDE OF THE PEAK DISTRICT
DERBYSHIRE INNS - an A to Z guide
HALLS AND CASTLES OF THE PEAK DISTRICT & DERBYSHIRE
TOURING THE PEAK DISTRICT & DERBYSHIRE BY CAR
DERBYSHIRE FOLKLORE
PUNISHMENT IN DERBYSHIRE
CUSTOMS OF THE PEAK DISTRICT & DERBYSHIRE
WINSTER - a souvenir guide
ARKWRIGHT OF CROMFORD
LEGENDS OF DERBYSHIRE
DERBYSHIRE FACTS & RECORDS
TALES FROM THE MINES by Geoffrey Carr
PEAK DISTRICT PLACE NAMES by Martin Spray
DERBYSHIRE THROUGH THE AGES - Vol 1 -DERBYSHIRE IN PREHISTORIC TIMES
SIR JOSEPH PAXTON
FLORENCE NIGHTINGALE
JOHN SMEDLEY
BONNIE PRINCE CHARLIE & 20 mile walk.
THE STORY OF THE EARLS AND DUKES OF DEVONSHIRE

JOHN MERRILL'S MAJOR WALKS -

TURN RIGHT AT LAND'S END
WITH MUSTARD ON MY BACK
TURN RIGHT AT DEATH VALLEY
EMERALD COAST WALK
I CHOSE TO WALK - Why I walk etc.
A WALK IN OHIO - 1,310 miles around the Buckeye Trail.
I AM GUIDED - the story of John's life.

SKETCH BOOKS -

SKETCHES OF THE PEAK DISTRICT

COLOUR BOOK:-

THE PEAK DISTRICT.......something to remember her by.

OVERSEAS GUIDES -

HIKING IN NEW MEXICO - Vol I - The Sandia and Manzano Mountains.
Vol 2 - Hiking "Billy the Kid" Country.
Vol 4 - N.W. area - " Hiking Indian Country."
"WALKING IN DRACULA COUNTRY" - Romania.
WALKING THE TRAILS OF THE HONG KONG ISLANDS.

VISITOR GUIDES - MATLOCK . BAKEWELL. ASHBOURNE.

See all my books on -
www.johnmerrillwalkguides.co.uk

Pilgrim guides -
www.thejohnmerrillministry.co.uk

Wherever you are, you are either

on or close to a

John Merrill Walk.

........enjoy!

May the sun bring you new energy by day,
May the moon softly restore you by night,
May the rain wash away your worries,
May the breeze blow new strength into your being,
May you walk gently through the world and
Know it's beauty all the days of your life.

Apache blessing.

Look at the tees,
Look at the birds,
Look at the clouds,
Look at the stars ....
And if you have eyes
you will be able to see
that the whole of
existence is joyful.

Osho

THE JOHN MERRILL MINISTRY
- a universal monk -
embracing & honouring
all faiths & none.

John has been following his own spiritual path all his life, and is guided. He was brought up as a Christian and confirmed at the age of 13. He then went to a Quaker Boarding School for five years and developed his love for the countryside and walking. He became fascinated with Tibet and whilst retaining his Christian roots, became immersed in Buddhism. For four years he studied at the Tara Buddhist Centre in Derbyshire. He progressed into Daoism and currently attends the Chinese Buddhist Temple (Pure Land Tradition) in London. With his thirst for knowledge and discovery he paid attention to other faiths and appreciated their values. Late in life he decided it was time to reveal his spiritual beliefs and practices and discovered the Interfaith Seminary.

'When the pupil is ready, the teacher will appear'. (Buddhist saying).

Here for two years he learnt in more depth the whole spectrum of faiths , including Jainism, Paganism, Mother Earth, Buddhism, Hinduism, Islam, Judaism, Sikhism, Celtic Worship and Shamanism. This is an ongoing exploration without end. He embraces all faiths, for all have a beauty of their own. All paths/faiths lead to one goal/truth. On July 17th. 2010 he was Ordained as a Multi-faith Minister.

'May you go in peace, with joy in your heart
and may the divine be always at your side.'

Using his knowledge and experience he combines many faiths into a simple, caring and devoted services, individually made for each specific occasion, with dignity and honour.
He conducts special Ceremonies -

Popular Funeral Celebrant and member of the Natural Death Society.

* Funerals * Memorial Services * Sermons * Weddings   *Civil Partnerships
* Baby Blessings & Naming
* Rites of Passage * Healing Ceremonies * Pilgimages * Inspirational Talks
Qigong Teacher.   Reiki Prationer.

For further information Contact John on -
Tel/Fax: 01992 - 762776 Mobile. 07910 889429
Email - universalmonk@oulook.com
Ministry site -www.thejohnmerrillministry.co.uk
All Faiths church - www.londoninterfaithchurch.co.uk

Revd. John N. Merrill, HonMUni
32, Holmesdale, Waltham Cross,
Hertfordshire EN8 8QY